CHICAGO: A Pictorial History

CHICAGO A PICTORIAL HISTORY

by HERMAN KOGAN
and LLOYD WENDT

BONANZA BOOKS · NEW YORK

Library of Congress Catalog Number: 58-11914

*This edition published by Bonanza Books,
a division of Crown Publishers, Inc.,
by arrangement with E. P. Dutton and Company, Inc.*
D E F G H

PREVIOUS BOOKS
In Collaboration:

LORDS OF THE LEVEE

BET A MILLION!

GIVE THE LADY WHAT SHE WANTS

BIG BILL OF CHICAGO

By LLOYD WENDT:

GUNNERS GET GLORY

BRIGHT TOMORROW

By HERMAN KOGAN:

THE GREAT E B

UNCOMMON VALOR (collaborator)

SEMPER FIDELIS (contributor)

Facing title page

Modern Chicago, looking northeast toward Lake Michigan from the U. S. Postoffice across the downtown district of office buildings, factories, stores, warehouses and skyscrapers. *(Chicago Tribune.)*

Front end papers

Marvel of the age in the late 1850s was the Chicago that sprawled by Lake Michigan. In little more than two decades it had bloomed from a swamp town into a city of nearly 100,000, proudly asserting its regal rights as "Queen of the Lakes." I. T. Palmatary, a well-known artist of that era, worked for months to make this meticulously detailed "View of Chicago"—complete with pictorial prophecies about schooners arriving from Liverpool—and delighted citizens bought copies at $12.00 each. *(Richard Richard.)*

Rear end papers

Chicago in 1958: A view looking north toward the Loop skyscraper district at upper right. In the foreground extending the width of the photograph is the new Congress Street highway, cutting through the Post Office just after it crosses the south branch of the Chicago River. *(Al Madsen, Chicago Tribune.)*

Contents

FOREWORD   vii

ONE HUNDRED YEARS AGO   10

IN THE BEGINNING, A CROSSING PLACE   38

FORT DEARBORN AND THE MASSACRE   50

CANAL AND BOOM TOWN   63

THE BOOMERS AND BOOSTERS   75

"QUEEN OF THE NORTH AND THE WEST"   89

THE GREAT FIRE   115

MIDLAND METROPOLIS   131

"THAT WINDY CITY"   157

PLANS, WARS AND POLITICS   187

FROM FAIR TO FAIR   206

INDEX   222

Foreword

The responsibility for *Chicago: A Pictorial History* is, of course, our own. But we must here acknowledge our inestimable debt to those who were helpful to us in our quest for illustrations and in our preparation of text.

The list is long and varied, ranging from old settlers and private collectors of Chicagoana and booksellers to scholars, librarians, and photographers. We are especially grateful to Miss Elizabeth Baughman, Mrs. Mary Frances Rhymer, Miss Elaine Sawyer, Grant Dean for their assistance to us in locating materials in the archives of the Chicago Historical Society. Similar aid was given us by Herbert Hewitt and his industrious staff in the reference department of the Chicago Public Library. Counsel and advice especially valuable came from Dr. Bessie Louise Pierce, whose multi-volumed *A History of Chicago* is the definitive work in this field, and Milo Quaife, prime authority on Chicago's earliest history.

Walter Scholl made available to us his unique and fascinating picture collection and Eugene I. Stein, Jr. allowed full access to the copious files of Kaufmann and Fabry, the firm of which he is president. We are grateful, too, for aid and assistance from many of our colleagues in the photographic departments of the *Chicago Sun-Times* and the *Chicago Tribune;* from officials in charge of libraries maintained by Chicago industrial firms and civic groups, and from Joseph Benson, head of the Chicago Municipal Reference Library. Other libraries from which we obtained pictorial and textual data include those in the Art Institute of Chicago, Northwestern University, and the University of Chicago, Newberry Library, and the Library of Congress, the New York Public Library, and the libraries of the *New York Times* and the Illinois Historical Society.

The creations of individual artists, sketchers, etchers, and photographers have been, so far as is possible, identified as they appear in the pages that follow. It has been an authentic pleasure for us to witness, as we selected from their works, the development of a city of which we are fond.

HERMAN KOGAN
LLOYD WENDT

CHICAGO: A Pictorial History

One Hundred Years Ago

All that sweltering summer of 1858 the country's eyes were on Chicago.

Elsewhere factories were shut, steamers lay idle, and men stood in bread lines. Almost alone of the thousands of communities felled by the panic of 1857, Chicago was recovering. Schooners creaked in their berths along the cluttered Chicago River. Dock hands stacked gleaming piles of Wisconsin and Michigan pine beside the slips, rolled out barrels of packed pork for the barges bound to New Orleans. High above the river reeking with the offal of a dozen packing plants chain belts of the elevators clanked, moving 9,000,000 bushels of wheat, 7,500,000 bushels of corn this depression-ridden year.

To the east, on the north bank of the river, 2,000 workmen trudged to their jobs in the great McCormick Reaper Works, turning out the 4,000 machines that would reach the western harvest fields that year. Locomotives—a dozen, two dozen, a hundred—rattled into the yards and along the spurs, snorting their defiance of all panics and all rivals, such older cities as St. Louis, Cincinnati, Buffalo, and Toledo, towns soon to be left behind.

Chicago was twenty-five that summer, with a population of 90,000 spraddling the Lake Michigan marshlands. There had been panic: all but two of the banks failed, fortunes lost on corner lots, 3,000 discouraged residents fleeing elsewhere. There had been pestilence: cholera from the sodden streets and stinking marshes claimed citizens by the hundreds. There had been fire: twenty-one dead in a roaring blaze that swept

Lake and Water streets clean of stores, warehouses, rooming houses, and upstairs brothels.

Yet now Chicago was rising again, flaunting civic slogans, rebuilding Lake Street, literally lifting itself from the mud on thousands of jackscrews. In this remarkable year just a century ago the slab town was calling for workers, calling for capital at 18 and 20 per cent, calling for railroad cars and bottoms to haul the wheat and fetch supplies. Only twenty-five years before this braggart city had been a mudhole trading post of wigwams and log huts. Now it boldly forecast a population of 2,000,000 by the turn of the century and announced its plans for a giant fair in 1859, an exhibition intended, once and for all, to establish Chicago's leadership of the Northwest, its right to rule as Queen of the Lakes.

From rival towns and friendly towns reporters came to observe, to scoff, to marvel. *Hunt's Merchants' Magazine* of New Orleans was convinced: "Chicago is booming again! Its future seems assured." Said *Ballou's Pictorial Drawing Room Companion* in Boston: "There is no doubt of it. Chicago is the greatest grain market in the world and chief commercial emporium of the Northwest." In New York, *Harper's Weekly* declared: "Chicago, the entrepôt for the grain trade of the Northwest, is the first point at which recovery is felt."

John Delane, editor of the *London Times,* inspected the scattered stockyards, climbed the great elevators on the river front, and exclaimed: "It is incredible that such a city could be built

Left. A strident symbol of Chicago in 1858: Mayor "Long John" Wentworth, who first boosted the city, then himself. His investment in city property made him wealthy; his flamboyant ways made him nationally famous. *(Chicago Antiquities.)*

Above. Pride of the young town a century ago was its courthouse of Lockport limestone, set in the central square bounded by Randolph, Clark, Washington, and La Salle streets. Citizens took visitors to its tower promenade to view the sights. And from that lofty perch Alexander Hesler, famed as a daguerreotype expert, photographed Chicago's portrait as shown on the following pages. *(Chicago Historical Society.)*

in so few years." Even rival Cincinnati conceded the new Chicago boom. "This is no swamp town," said its *Inquirer,* "it is a metropolis with a future. The Chicago boosters will not be held back."

There were dissenters. "Chicago is nothing but hovels and a stench behind a façade of brick and marble store fronts," wrote a Buffalo journalist. "An impoverished city with no future, reveling in an orgy of crime," insisted the *St. Louis Post.* "Chicago is merely a windy place, where the principal productions are corner lots, statistics, and Long John Wentworth," pronounced the *Cleveland Plain Dealer.*

In this vital year Chicago was ruled by a tall, lean, hot-tempered former Democrat who had joined the new Republicans and led them in a clean sweep of all Cook county and city offices. "Long John" Wentworth was, by any measure, a top man among the boosters. Twenty-two years before he had walked into town, a gangling six feet six of New Hampshire determination, his Dartmouth diploma in his carpetbag. Now he owned the *Daily Democrat* and 2,500 acres of Mud Lake land southwest of town. As the youngest member of Congress in 1843, he had been the hardest fighter for Chicago and the Northwest. In one year

11

CHICAGO SITS FOR A FIRST PORTRAIT. When Alexander Hesler packed his camera to the courthouse tower, fifty-eight feet above the central square, he achieved a series of panoramic views unparalleled for their time. In the foreground of what was then Chicago's business and entertainment area is the Sherman House, flanked on the left by Randolph Street saloons. At the southeast corner of Clark and Lake streets, one block north of Randolph Street, is the famous Saloon Building, Chicago's first city hall and office building erected in 1836. Along Lake Street can be seen some of the town's leading stores and part of the reconstruction that was being done after a fire in 1857.

At lower right a crew can be seen laying down wood blocks as part of the Clark Street paving project. In Randolph Street, around the corner to the right, are the theaters and concert saloons, above them the offices of prominent lawyers.

The cupola at the extreme right tops the Matteson Hotel at Dearborn and Randolph streets; each of the city's hotels had such cupolas, in which men sat with telescopes to spy out incoming boats and trains, to which omnibuses were swiftly dispatched. To the left of the Matteson Hotel a higher and grander cupola designates the Tremont House, then the best known of the city's hostelries.

In the background along the Chicago River are the grain elevators on its banks and many vessels, whose spars are clearly visible from the courthouse tower. *Chicago Historical Society*

Canadian-born Alexander Hesler accompanied his parents to Racine, Wisconsin, in 1833. After four years as a clerk, Hesler learned daguerreotyping at Buffalo, New York, in only ten days, set up a studio at Madison, Wisconsin, and later Galena. He came to Chicago in 1853; won international honors for his work. He died in Evanston, Illinois, in 1895. *(Chicago Tribune Library.)*

as mayor he had personally led a raid that destroyed The Sands, the north-side vice center; raided the premises of downtown businessmen who ignored his order to remove signs and rubble from the sidewalks; and fired the entire police department in a fit of anger. True, the exasperated citizens interrupted Long John's reign in March 1858 by electing Republican John Haines mayor, but the country still thought of Chicago as Wentworth's town.

Despite the raids, Chicago was ugly, dirty, noisy, and crime-ridden. Prostitutes, gamblers, and thugs driven from The Sands scattered about the town, or regrouped in Gamblers' Alley, a district of shacks and hovels a block south of the city hall. Visitors arriving on the Illinois Central found themselves carried downtown over a series of mud flats on giant piers strung along the lake front. Land promoters, porters, hack drivers, omnibus men from the hotels yelled, fought, and jostled as they descended on incoming passengers in the station yard, hurrying to snare a solvent client before a pickpocket robbed him. Nearby, the river was cluttered with ships and barges, blasting for right of way or the bridges to open. And lining the river were huge elevators where steam lifts wheezed, packing plants with their pens of squealing pigs and bawling cattle, and warehouses beside their private docks, swarming with stevedores who unloaded lumber, hardware, barrels of sugar, molasses, rum, and whisky.

Chicago lay low, only two feet above the river, except where the fills had been made and George M. Pullman was raising the buildings on his jackscrews. Wooden drains and wooden walks had rotted and collapsed. Visitors stepping on them were greeted by a spray of mud and scurrying rats. The wealthier residents had escaped to higher ground on Terrace Row, or north of the river where they maintained handsome homes amid orchards and gardens. But the denizens of Kilgubbin, Conley's Patch, and Hardscrabble dwelt in mud and filth, their rickety shacks teetering on stilts. In dry weather the visitor was assailed by stench and dust. In wet weather his carriage might sink to the hubs in a main street and the stench was no more bearable.

14

Looking southeast from the courthouse tower, Hesler's camera caught the city's downtown churches and swept on to the residential area along Michigan Avenue and Terrace Row on the lake front. To the rear of Bryant & Stratton's National Mercantile College is the steeple of the Unitarian Church whose bell tolled at 6 A.M., noon, and 6 P.M. In the center background is St. Mary's Catholic Church, with the Methodist Church under construction at the lower right. Clustered beyond this partly-built structure are the houses and shacks of Gambler's Row, chief retreat of the city's unsavory elements after Mayor Wentworth raided The Sands in 1857. Across from this patch of vice and crime is the shell of the United States Post Office and Customs Building. The tall spire in the distance off to the upper right is that of the Plymouth Congregational Church at Ninth Street and Wabash Avenue; later, after the Great Fire of 1871, it became Old St. Mary's Catholic Church. *(Chicago Historical Society.)*

Caroline Kirkland looked upon it all and wrote:

Chicago is the grandest, flattest, muddiest, dustiest, hottest, coldest, wettest, driest place in the world. It has the best harbor on Lake Michigan, and the worst harbor and smallest river any great commercial city ever lived on. . . . It has the most elegant architecture, the meanest hovels, the wildest speculation, the solidest values. It is proudest in self-esteem, and loudest in self-disparagement. . . . Chicago, the wondrous, sits amid her wealth, like a magnificent Sultana, half-reclining over a great oval mirror . . . but we are told that Oriental beauties, with all their splendor, are not especially clean.

Yet there was a beauty and a promise seen most clearly by the boosters. John Stephen Wright was one of them; he was only forty-three, yet he had won and lost two fortunes in Chicago and now was spending his last dollars pamphleteering his praises of the town. And Long John Wentworth, and William Ogden, builder of canals and railroads, whose word alone brought the town a million dollars in foreign loans. And Deacon William Bross, big and brassy, part prophet and part editor, who roared:

Chicago's territory is bigger than twenty-three states. It contains the largest and richest deposits of lead and copper on the globe. Where the buffalo now range must, after all, become the greatest corn-growing section of the Union. There, too, will be reared the countless herds of cattle and hogs to be driven to Chicago and pack in as beef and pork to feed the Eastern states, with an abundance to spare for all the nations of Europe!

These indomitable men had been hit hard by the panic, Wright crushed by it when he backed his Atkins reaping machine with his fortune. There were scores more, men who scraped their tills and mortgaged their lives to build again, to organize their great fair.

Although corn was down to 30 cents a bushel, wheat to 58, oats to 24, and eggs sold for 10 cents a dozen, Chicago in this year spent $3,000,-000 on new structures in the business area, $418,000 on street paving, built three new bridges to bring the total to 16, welcomed its tenth railroad—the Pittsburgh, Ft. Wayne and Chicago—

Another Hesler view looking down upon Washington Street, with Clark Street at the left and La Salle Street at the right. Mechanics Institute Hall, at lower left, had been the First Presbyterian Church; here Chicago's young men attended lectures on science, politics, and philosophy, and inspected agricultural and mechanical arts exhibitions. In this year, business houses were starting to encroach on Clark Street's residential blocks. At upper center is the city's water tank, which survived the Great Fire of 1871 and was then used first as a temporary city hall and later as a public library.

South along La Salle Street, with the First Baptist Church in the foreground, are tree-lined blocks with fashionable homes. But to the west, on the Chicago River, is a squalid slum packed with immigrants, a region of cheap saloons, water-front fights to which police were summoned nightly. The building with the segmented roof in left center is Levi J. North's amphitheater, where a circus appeared in summer and mammoth theatrical pageants were offered in winter. This sector of La Salle Street is now Chicago's financial district, with the Board of Trade Building towering high over a canyon of skyscrapers on the site of an 1858 rooming house. *(Chicago Historical Society.)*

This clutter of woodsheds, livery stables, and cheap hotels was caught by Hesler as he turned his camera westward toward the south branch of the Chicago River. A piano dealer occupied the four-story building on La Salle Street in the foreground. At the upper right is the five-story Lind Block, which survived the Great Fire of 1871 and still stands today, and across from it, on the northeast corner, the Star Saloon, so capacious that prize fights could be staged and town bands could rehearse there. *(Chicago Historical Society.)*

Before making his unprecedented views from the courthouse tower, Hesler poked about in other spots. Here is a very rare photograph of the rebuilt Fort Dearborn, then serving as a government hospital, taken from across the Chicago River. (*Chicago Historical Society.*)

laid tracks for its first bobtail horse railroad in State Street, greeted 6,882 vessels which carried $27,194,114 in lake and canal imports. No longer did droves of cattle pound the Rush Street bridge, or Conestoga drivers camp along the lake front, for new stockyards were opened on the south and west sides. The largest, on the Southwestern Plank Road, was established by Matthew Laflin to provide drovers as customers for his Bull's Head Tavern, and the combination helped to make him rich.

It was a year of extremes. "No city on earth has increased as rapidly in wealth and population," said *Frank Leslie's Weekly*. "Chicago is one of the most miserable and ugly cities I have yet seen in America," wrote Fredrika Bremer, the Swedish author. There was criminality. "Chicago is certainly winning her way to a front rank in the scale of criminal society," grimly admitted the *Daily Democrat*. It was a year, too, of religious revival. If Chicago's 541 saloons were busy, so were its 70 churches. Daily revival meetings were held, in churches, halls, theaters, tents. More than 3,000 persons attended noon prayer sessions in Metropolitan Hall, packing it and the street. "I attend a Baptist church where there is a great congregation," Alexander Leslie, a newly arrived Scot, recorded in his diary. "Most of the churches are open every day, and thousands collect for the noon prayer services. Religion and politics take everyone's attention. There are so many Germans here some of the political meetings are conducted in English and German."

Political interest soared when Senator Stephen

A later photograph by Hesler of the Lake House, now cut off from Lake Michigan by rooming houses and other new buildings. In the foreground is the Rush Street swing bridge which replaced the earlier ferry, and a portion of one of the lumberyards that lined miles of river front and made Chicago a foremost lumber market. *(Chicago Historical Society.)*

A. Douglas, Chicago's stalwart "Little Giant," returned home July 9. Douglas had broken with President Buchanan over the slavery strife in Kansas, and abolitionist Chicago welcomed him wildly as he began his campaign for re-election. Nearly 30,000 heard Douglas speak from a Tremont House balcony after day-long parading in his honor. The following day, Abraham Lincoln, Douglas' Republican opponent, spoke from the same balcony, to a smaller but equally enthusiastic crowd. Chicago was a center of abolitionist activity: it sent supplies to the Free Soilers in Kansas, it maintained an important terminus of the underground railroad, its press waged an incessant attack on slavery. Chicago had welcomed Douglas so uproariously partly out of local pride, partly because he now wanted Kansas to enter the Union as a free state, and partly because he paid the

costs of his homecoming celebration himself. In November, Chicago voted Republican.

This 1858 was the year of opportunity. "It is the place for a poor man," wrote James Lawrence, a plasterer from Rye Neck, New York, to his wife, Sarah. "Here is the place where a man can be free. In a year or two I will save enough for a farm. Our children can get a good education for nothing. I would not go back to the poorhouse in Westchester County."

"You must come," Lawrence pleaded in a later letter. "This is a Christian community. We have churches and revivals and lots of Sabbath schools. If you was here the children could go to day school free of cost.

"We could all live well here. I could get much more work if I could take some of my pay in groceries. I pay $3.00 a week for my board and room in a house (at 75 West Monroe Street) where they pay $12.00 a month rent. I leave at four in the morning, and get home at six in the afternoon. I do plastering on a mammoth factory building and I get $1.50 a day. You would like it here. There are no snakes. If you would take one look at these beautiful prairies, all your sadness would flee."

Within the year, Lawrence had found a new job, a political patronage job. "My work is easy," he wrote. "I work as inspector of brick in public works and I get $15.00 a week! I ought to make enough money in a year or two for a house and lot. I am sending you the money for boat passage—it is better than trains and you can carry more baggage."

Others found themselves fitting snugly into the life of the flourishing town. The Irish were courted by Douglas and became Democrats. The Germans and Scandinavians joined with the new Republicans. Soon the voices of the foreign-born would be decisive in the town's elections and names of their favorite sons would balance off the rival political tickets.

Chicago in that year was a town of lonely young men. "The streets are very peculiar in not having a lady walking in them," wrote Caroline Kirkland. "But there are crowds of men from the greenest rustic, or the most undisguised sharper, to the man of most serious respectability." Many of the men lost their money in the gambling dens, spent it in the saloons and concert halls, and helped maintain the vice industry of 110 brothels, 40 houses of assignation, and 1,000 women, ruled

The first church building in Chicago was St. Mary's, a frame structure on Lake Street erected by the Rev. John Mary Ireneaus St. Cyr in 1833. Later, in 1843, this larger edifice was built at Madison Street and Wabash Avenue, opening for services on Christmas Day. It became the cathedral for the Chicago diocese, established the same year to embrace all of Illinois. (Paulist Fathers.)

Hot-tempered "Long John" Wentworth was ever a man of action, firm and direct and often drastic. After his raid on The Sands destroyed the town's vice district on the banks of the Chicago River, he ordered businessmen and vendors to clear their sidewalks of their signs and rubble. When they lagged in fulfilling this command, Wentworth conducted another raid, with results graphically depicted in *Frank Leslie's Illustrated Weekly,* whose Chicago agent, incidentally, was one of the victims of Wentworth's ire. *(Chicago Historical Society.)*

by a former prostitute who called herself Julia Freelove. To combat the evils, Cyrus Bentley and his friends organized the Young Men's Christian Association and set up reading rooms over Titsworth's store. Dwight L. Moody, a former shoe salesman, organized the Illinois Street mission to divert boys from sinful ways, and the Presbyterians opened their railroad mission among immigrants on the near south side.

But there were ladies of refinement and respectability in Chicago, many thousands of them. They did get about downtown, and they were helping the merchants on Lake Street to make fast recovery from the panic. They crowded into Potter Palmer's elegant new store where, he advertised, "possessing facilities not enjoyed by any other firm in the Trade, I am prepared to offer DRY goods at less price than any other house in the city." And Palmer's competitors, T. B. Carter & Co., M. & T. Doherty, Titsworth's, M. P. Ross & Co., and many others were doing well, too.

The ladies were buying enormous lengths of yard goods for their crinolines, French gloves, whalebone, "Kiss-Me-Quick" pomades and soaps, Pistachio nut skin and complexion powder, copies of *Uncle Tom's Cabin* by Mrs. Harriet Beecher Stowe, DuPuy's perfume from Paris and Frangipangi perfume from Rome.

The ladies shone splendidly at the dances

staged almost nightly by one or another of the town's fire companies, lodges, or military organizations. Alexander Leslie attended a Sons of Malta ball in the glittering new McVicker's Theater, and wrote in his diary: "Beauties of every hue flittered in the mazes of the shifting dance and hundreds of fair ones attired in elegant costumes of every color of the rainbow mingled with somber black coats in the glare of a thousand lights." Few social distinctions were maintained. Servant girls danced with rising young lawyers. "Many of the girls in domestic service come from good families and make excellent marriages," Leslie observed. Dancing, he added, was a passion in Chicago. He attended a social supper in a north side mansion. "There was polite small talk until we sat at supper. Then it became clear that the ladies were eager for the dancing to begin, although most present were Methodists or Presbyterians."

Culture, too, reached the new town. Leonard W. Volk, the sculptor, arrived after study in Italy and that summer made a bust of Senator Douglas, who paid his tuition abroad, and one of Abraham Lincoln. Another to arrive was George P. A. Healy, portrait artist, who brought a formidable reputation as a painter of crowned heads and nobility in Europe and winner of a gold medal in the Universal Exhibition in Paris in 1855. Alexander Hesler was gaining national fame with his daguerreotypes. The great Karl Formes came to Metropolitan Hall to conduct a chorus of 60 in Haydn's Oratorio of the Creation. Carl Anshuts organized a Metropolitan Hall orchestra and Chicagoans had their first opera season, opening with *La Somnambula.* There were lectures almost every night at the Mechanics' Institute. McVicker's Theater opened with a resident stock company which presented *Facts and Fancies,* a ballad opera written by Chicagoans William

Many of the town's sidewalks were rickety and narrow and could be reached only by ladders or wooden stairways, as in this view of Clark Street south of Lake Street. On days when it rained heavily, many streets turned to seas of mud; a joke of the times told of a woman in crinoline who toppled from such a walk into a mud-filled street and disappeared "under full sail." *(Chicago Historical Society.)*

Toothe and William H. Curie. "It was a very neat trifle, it cannot presume to be more, but worth repetition," said the *Democrat*. The Chicago Theater on Dearborn Street, the German Theater, and North's National Amphitheater presented actors and concert artists, Swiss bell ringers, animal acts. Three minstrel companies performed in the theaters or the concert saloons on Randolph Street: Frank Lombard's, Frank Peel's, and Miss Lucrete's Female Minstrels.

The new Chicago Historical Society, organized in 1856, attracted the solid citizens of the town to its lecture meetings. The Chicago Academy of Sciences was seeking funds for a museum, and doctors at Rush Medical College were organizing the Chicago Academy of Medical Sciences. Ladies dragged their husbands to concerts by the Chicago Amateur Orchestra Club and to occasional men's nights of the Mendelssohn Literary Association or the Kinzie Literary Club. *Sloan's Weekly,* a literary review, briefly filled a void ignored by

the city's 11 daily and weekly newspapers. Chicago boasted a high school, 109 grade schools, 13 Catholic parochial schools, Rush Medical College, Northwestern University and Female Institute in Evanston, the University of Chicago, the College of St. Mary's of the Lake, and four theological seminaries. There were four hospitals and 11 public halls.

The men, for the most part, were too preoccupied with business and politics to pay much attention to culture. Their social lives were largely organized by the lodges, fire companies, and military groups to which they belonged. Among the elite were the military organizations, the Highland Guards, Chicago Dragoons, Chicago Light Guards, Montgomery Guards, and Washington Independents. The fire companies, once enjoying high status, were falling into disrepute. Three companies, responding to a blaze at Fulton and Jefferson on the night of July 2, permitted their social rivalries to flare so high that a riot ensued. The

When, in the 1850s, Chicago started to climb out of its mud, the man who showed the way was young George M. Pullman. He convinced Ira Couch, proprietor of the Tremont House, that the hotel could be lifted eight feet "without disturbing a guest or cracking a cup." Pullman so successfully carried out this feat—using 500 men and 2,500 jackscrews—that other similar assignments were given him. A *Harper's Weekly* artist recorded this raising of another hotel, the Briggs House. *(Chicago Historical Society.)*

Crinolines were the rage in 1858. Many Chicago ladies visited the stores on Lake Street, especially Potter Palmer's new five-story, marble-front establishment, to shop for whalebone and yards of dress goods for their seamstresses to convert into stunning gowns such as these pictured in the *Ladies' Journal. (Chicago Historical Society.)*

volunteer firemen battled one another while a four-story brick furniture factory, a planing mill, a lumberyard, and several workers' shanties burned at a loss of $20,000.

"It is not determined who started the fight, but companies Nos. II, VI, and XIX were in the melee," the *Press and Tribune* reported. "The quarrel appears to have started from a shortage of hose lines. At one point Companies VI and XIX invited Company II to have a drink, but the latter refused, attacking with iron spanners.

"There is little doubt that whisky was the prime mover in the affray. Steam engines do not drink whisky or strike with spanners. En route back, No. XIX was attacked by rowdies who belong to No. VIII. The police should find these rowdy firemen and see that they are punished."

No errant firemen were found, however, save for Fritz Pieler, of No. II, who was taken to a hospital with a split skull.

Through 1859, Chicago's new boom continued, led by the ten railroads hauling more than five times as much wheat, hides, and wool as the canal and lake combined. The railroads had captured all the cotton cargoes and most of the cured meats. They carried double the tonnage of merchandise and sundries hauled in bottoms, and left water shipping supreme only in lumber, iron, and coal. Still, lake and canal commerce prospered. In a forty-eight-hour period 77 vessels arrived in the port of Chicago, the lumber schooners laying

An artist's graphic jest about the ladies' fashions of the period, styles which were assiduously followed by the well-to-do females of the Chicago of 1858. *Harper's Weekly* titled this drawing: "NEW CONTRIVANCE OF LADIES' MAIDS, Adapted to the Present Style of Fashions." *(Chicago Historical Society.)*

Dashing young men and their ladies picnicked, went on sleigh rides, danced the quadrille, and, at some evening parties, played a stimulating game of Fox and Geese. *(Harper's Weekly.)*

Skating was a most popular winter sport, and those who could afford it used the vast covered rink at Wabash Avenue and Jackson Street, where hot coffee and chocolate could be had and a German band played lively tunes. *(Chicago Public Library.)*

More daring were the jaunts to stagecoach inns outside Chicago, where a sumptuous supper of game could be had after a bracing ride. Even a husking bee on a nearby farm was far from dull, for the man who found a red ear could always collect a kiss, or he could try. *(Chicago Historical Society.)*

down 6,000,000 board feet of pine and fir. Lake trade with Canada was rising, and vessels from Europe brought manufactures, returning with wheat, packed pork, and beef.

From the ruins of panic Chicago was rising as a wholesale and manufacturing center on a greater scale than before. There were thirty-four wholesale houses in business, six clothing manufacturers, and a dozen more processing hides into shoes, belts, and saddlery. Fourteen elevating warehouses, with a capacity of 4,155,000 bushels of storage, were in operation. Along Lake Street the retail stores expanded, as the railroads made shopping trips from the hinterland possible.

Chicago poured work and its sparse funds into the upcoming United States Fair and Seventh Annual Exhibition of the United States Agricultural Society. A 45-acre tract was set aside on the lake front south of town, at the terminus of the new double-tracked horse railroad being laid at top speed in State Street. There W. W. Rovington directed the creation of an exposition city around a 40-foot-wide turf track and inside a larger concourse intended for the carriages of visitors. Six exhibition buildings went up, plus stables for horses and mules, with 800 stalls, cattle and sheep barns, corrals for livestock. The two new telegraph companies in town strung their wires to a press headquarters building. A restaurant was built near the fair's grand entrance on Cottage Grove Avenue.

The formal opening of the fair on September 13, 1859, saw Chicago packed with visitors. The railroads alone brought in more than 5,000 in 84 coaches the first day, convincing proof of Chicago's accessibility. Thousands more arrived over the plank roads and by boat. Public schools were closed for the week and it was estimated that more than 60,000 proud Chicagoans and their guests lined the streets for the opening parade to the fairgrounds.

Captain Charles Barker's resplendent Dragoons, the official escort, led the procession, which included fourteen militia companies and twenty bands. Most of the town's drays and vans were converted to floats depicting facets of Chi-

In the summer of 1858 Abraham Lincoln of Springfield clashed with Chicago's "Little Giant," Stephen A. Douglas, in a senatorial contest fraught with grave implications for the divided country. A few months earlier, Lincoln posed for a portrait (below) by Hesler. He rumpled his hair, saying he would not be recognized any other way. Douglas won re-election, after the series of Lincoln-Douglas debates. (*Meserve Collection.*)

Stephen A. Douglas thrived
as politician and landowner.

Potter Palmer, who knew how
to please the ladies.

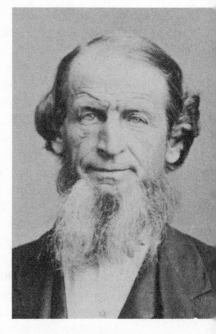

John Van Osdel, architect,
designed the courthouse.

John B. Rice. His theaters
were the finest in Chicago.

A top Chicago booster was
William Bross, the "Deacon."

Sculptor Leonard Volk, who
brought culture to town.

cago's greatness. Prize stallions, cattle, even flocks of sheep were in the line of march. Triumphantly the procession moved to the fairgrounds corrals, while outside the gates military salutes were fired and pyrotechnics set off. Professor Arnold Steiner soared on a hot-air balloon ascension, and excursion boats and beflagged pleasure craft staged a regatta offshore. The crowds pressed into the exhibit halls, seeing entire gardens transplanted, kitchens equipped with the latest in stoves, cistern pumps, coffee grinders, and washing machines. On they moved to Power Hall, where steam engines turned lathes, saws, and planers, and into the agricultural machinery exhibit, jammed with plows, reapers, mowers, corn shellers, binders, grain separators, and even a full-scale replica of a sleeping car for drovers' trains—a cumbersome caboose lined with detachable bunks.

Big events in addition to the daily horse races were the band concerts, the fire-company competitions, and the contest for the supremacy of the steam plows, reserved for the third day. Two enormous entries excited public imagination. James Waters' lumbering giant, brought in from Detroit, was pulled by an 18-foot steam engine and totaled 55 feet in length. The second, built by Joseph W. Fawkes at Lancaster, Pennsylvania, was equally huge, a series of gang plows linked together by heavy chains and towed by an engine that had leading wheels five feet in diameter.

Thousands lined the testing field as the Waters machine snorted out first, coughing black smoke, groaning and squealing as the plowshares were lowered to take the turf. Within two minutes Waters had plowed one eighth of an acre as the crowd cheered. Then his engine choked and stalled, and disgustedly quit. A drag chain had broken. The timekeeper shouted that the plowing had been done at a rate of three and one-eighth acres an hour. Soon the Fawkes plow lumbered out. The chains creaked, the blades bit in, and seventeen minutes later an acre of fresh-turned turf lay before the yelling crowd. Fawkes won $3,000 and the fair's gold medal for his feat. The tough prairie sod had been conquered. Now the western plains would be opened at a pace no oxen could equal.

30

It was a week Chicago would remember. By the fourth day, 69,000 visitors had arrived, the greatest crowd in the history of the Northwest. More than 20,000 overflowed the hotels into private homes. The visitors got an extra thrill on the night of the fourth day when fire, one of 124 to hit Chicago in 1859, razed ten buildings at Canal and Lake. Despite this tragic finish, the fair was an unquestioned success. "It may be comforting to the croakers in less fortunate towns to know that Chicago's prosperity was never more real and solid," crowed the *Press and Tribune*. "There's no doubt of it, we exceed Cincinnati and St. Louis in every way!" exulted the *Herald,* Chicago's newest newspaper.

It was true that Chicago was moving into first place in the West. Not even the boosters guessed how soon dire events would help her actually to eclipse St. Louis and Cincinnati, border cities between the North and South. In October, mad John Brown marched on Harpers Ferry, and in December he was hanged. Chicago staged angry demonstrations, raised more money for the Free Soilers in Kansas, and voted Republican again. Few thought seriously of war. Chicago was too busy boosting and building, too preoccupied with pride in its rise from a wilderness mudhole only thirty years earlier. And many brash young hustlers in this roaring town would have been surprised to learn that its history began not thirty, nor fifty, but more than two hundred years before.

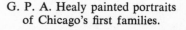

G. P. A. Healy painted portraits of Chicago's first families.

P. W. F. Peck. His store made
him a wealthy man.

Mayor John C. Haines took
Wentworth's city hall job.

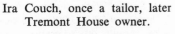

Ira Couch, once a tailor, later
Tremont House owner.

William B. Ogden was first
mayor and a railroad builder.

J. Young Scammon, a pioneer
banker and arts patron.

Panic and disaster did not stop Chicago. *Above*. In 1857, at the peak of the financial depression, fire razed the stores along Lake and South Water streets, costing 21 lives and $3,000,000. The stores were rebuilt on a grander scale within a year. *Left*. Railroad wrecks were frequent, such as this Michigan Southern derailment of an eastbound Chicago train in 1859, in which 44 passengers lost their lives. (*Frank Leslie's Illustrated Weekly*.)

Top. Chicago cheered the arrival of the *Madeira Pet* from Liverpool with
a cargo of crockery in 1857. It was the beginning of commerce with Europe.
The drawing appeared in the *Chicago Magazine* of 1857. *(Newberry Library.)*
Bottom. The Illinois and Michigan canal in downtown Chicago. Begun in
1836, completed in 1847, it linked the Gulf of Mexico with the Atlantic,
a project first urged by Louis Jolliet in 1673. *(Chicago Historical Society.)*

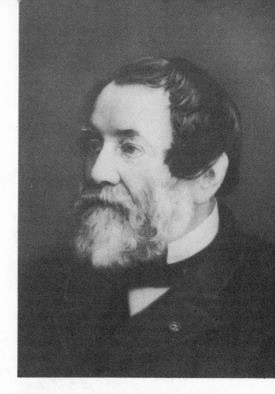

Mr. C. H. McCORMICK will please manufacture for the undersigned, and deliver at the Warehouse of   in   on or before the   day   , 1851, one of McCormick's last *Improved* Patent Virginia Reapers, (including three Fingers, three sections of the Sickle, and the Pinion extra,) for which the undersigned agrees to pay thirty dollars, and freight,(and Warehouse charges if any.)on delivery of said machine as aforesaid, and the further sum of ninety dollars on the first of December thereafter, with interest from the first day of July, 1851 : Provided that said Reaper will cut two acres of wheat or other small grain, in an hour ; that it will save at least three-fourths of all the wheat scattered by ordinary cradling ; that it is well made, of good material, and durable with proper care ; and that the raking of the wheat can be well done by a man riding upon it.

If, upon a fair trial, to be made next harvest, said Reaper cannot perform as above specified, and shall not be as above represented, the undersigned will lay it aside, and will store it safely, and re-deliver it to C. H. McCormick, subject to refunding the thirty dollars paid as above ; but if on trial said Reaper shall perform and be as above represented, the undersigned agrees when called on by said McCormick, or his Agent, to execute a Note for the balance of the purchase money, payable as aforesaid, at the

day of   , A. D., 1851.

Post Office address,

By 1858, Cyrus Hall McCormick's reaper plant on the north side of the river was making 4,000 machines a year. McCormick introduced installment buying, sold on a money-back guarantee. His 1851 order blank, shown here, provides for a $30.00 down payment, the balance of $90.00 on or after December 1. John S. Wright, manufacturing the Atkins reaper, sought to match McCormick's guarantee, lost $200,000 in 1857 when green wood warped and ruined his machines in the fields. (*International Harvester Company.*)

34

Despite fears of merchants that railroads would create rival shopping towns, their trade increased. Women, attracted by posters like these, used in 1858, looked forward to a Chicago shopping trip as a great event. *(Illinois Central.)* The Illinois Central station (right) was described as a marvel of the age. Situated on the lake front at the river, it was 504 feet long, 84 feet high, 166½ feet wide, accommodated eight tracks. *(Ballou's Pictorial Drawing Room Companion.)*

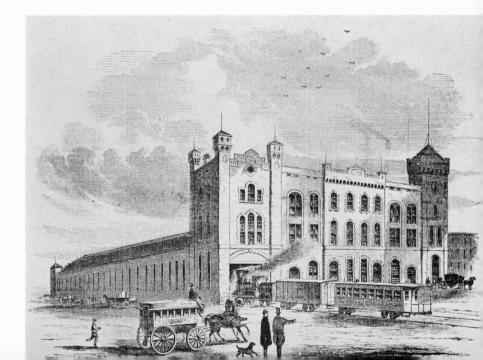

Railway workers were lured West by offers of good jobs and the opportunity to buy farm land cheap. An acreage could be bought for $24.00 down. *(Illinois Central.)*

ILLINOIS CENTRAL RAILROAD COMPANY
OFFER FOR SALE
ONE MILLION ACRES OF SUPERIOR FARMING LANDS,
IN FARMS OF
40, 80 & 160 acres and upwards at from $8 to $12 per acre.
THESE LANDS ARE
NOT SURPASSED BY ANY IN THE WORLD.
THEY LIE ALONG
THE WHOLE LINE OF THE CENTRAL ILLINOIS RAILROAD,
For Sale on LONG CREDIT, SHORT CREDIT and for CASH, they are situated near TOWNS, VILLAGES, SCHOOLS and CHURCHES.

For all Purposes of Agriculture.

The lands offered for sale by the Illinois Central Railroad Company are equal to any in the world. A healthy climate, a rich soil, and railroads to convey to market the fullness of the earth—all combine to place in the hands of the enterprising workingman the means of independence.

Illinois.

Extending 580 miles from North to South, has all the diversity of climate to be found between Massachusetts and Virginia, and varieties of soil adapted to the products of New England and those of the Middle States. The black soil in the central portions of the State is the richest known, and produces the finest corn, wheat, sorghum and hay, which latter crop, during the past year, has been highly remunerative. The selling of these prairie lands to tame grasses, for pastures, offers to farmers with capital the most profitable results. The smaller prairies interspersed with timber, in the more southern portion of the State, produce the best of winter wheat, tobacco, flax, hemp and fruit. The lands still farther South are heavily timbered, and here the raising of fruit, tobacco, cotton and the manufacture of lumber yield large returns. The health of Illinois is hardly surpassed by any State in the Union.

Grain and Stock Raising.

In the list of corn and wheat producing States, Illinois stands pre-eminently first. Its advantages for raising cattle and hogs are too well known to require comment here. For its upraising, the lands in every part of the State are well adapted, and Illinois can now boast of many of the largest flocks in the country. No branch in industry offers greater inducements for investment.

Hemp, Flax and Tobacco.

Hemp and flax easily produced of as good quality as any grown in Europe. Tobacco of the finest quality is raised upon lands purchased of this Company, and it promises to be one of the most important crops of the State. Cotton, too, is raised, to a considerable extent, in the southern portion. The making of sugar from the beet is receiving considerable attention, and experiments upon a large scale have been made during the past season. The cultivation of sorghum is rapidly increasing, and there are numerous indications that ere many years Illinois will produce a large surplus of sugar and molasses for exportation.

Fruit.

The central and southern parts of the State are peculiarly adapted to fruit raising ; and peaches, pears and strawberries, together with early vegetables, are sent to Chicago, St. Louis and Cincinnati, as well as other markets, and always command a ready sale.

Coal and Minerals.

The immense coal deposits of Illinois are worked at different points near the Railroad, and the great resources of the State in iron, lead, zinc, limestone, potters' clay, &c., &c., as yet barely touched, will eventually be the source of great wealth.

To Actual Settlers

the inducements offered are so great that the Company has already sold 1,500,000 acres, and the sales during the past year have been to a larger number of purchasers than ever before. The advantages to a man of small means, settling in Illinois, where his children may grow up with all the benefits of education and the best of public schools, can hardly be over-estimated. No State in the Union is increasing more rapidly in population, which has trebled in ten years along the line of this Railroad.

PRICES AND TERMS OF PAYMENT.

The price of land varies from $7 to $12 and upward per acre, and they are sold on long credit, on short credit, or for cash. A deduction of ten per cent. from the long credit price is made to those who make a payment of one-fourth of the principal down, and the balance in one, two, and three years. A deduction of **twenty per cent.** is made to those who purchase for cash. Never before have greater inducements been offered to cash purchasers.

EXAMPLE.

Forty acres at $10 per acre on long credit, interest at six per cent., payable annually in advance ; the principal in four, five, six, and seven years.

	INTEREST.	PRINCIPAL.		INTEREST.	PRINCIPAL.
Cash payment	$24.00		Cash payment	$16.20	$95.00
Payments in one year	24.00		Payment in one year	13.80	95.00
two years	24.00		two years	5.00	95.00
three "	24.00		three "		95.00
four "	18.00	$100.00			
five "	12.00	100.00			
six "	6.00	100.00			
seven "		100.00			

The same farm may be purchased for $320 in cash.

Full information on all points, together with maps, showing the exact location of the lands, will be furnished on application in person or by letter to

LAND COMMISSIONER,
Illinois Central R. R. Co., Chicago, Ill.

WANTED!
3,000 LABORERS
On the 12th Division of the
ILLINOIS CENTRAL RAILROAD
Wages, $1.25 per Day.
Fare, from New-York, only - - $4 75
By Railroad and Steamboat, to the work in the State of Illinois.

Constant employment for two years or more given. Good board can be obtained at two dollars per week.

This is a rare chance for persons to go West, being sure of permanent employment in a healthy climate, where land can be bought cheap, and for fertility is not surpassed in any part of the Union.

Men with families preferred.

For further information in regard to it, call at the Central Railroad Office.

173 BROADWAY,
CORNER OF COURTLANDT ST.
NEW-YORK.
R. B. MASON, Chief Engineer.
H. PHELPS, Agent.

Westward-bound passengers used this handsome new station of the Chicago and North Western Railroad on Kinzie Street, west of the north branch of the river. *(Chicago and North Western.)*

In the Beginning, a Crossing Place II

Glaciers powdered the coral reef, engraved a necklace of glittering lakes about the throat of a continent, left a rich black till, 75 feet deep, all the way to the Ozark hills. Then, dividing the land into east and west and north and south at Lake Chicago, the last great ice sheet retreated to its Laurentian uplands. The prairie bloomed with tall grasses and taller forests. Lake Chicago subsided into Lake Michigan, rimmed with sand dunes and potholes at its southern tip. Yet here, in the bleak marshlands, lay the continental divide. On the west the waters sought the southern sea. On the east they found a turbulent course to the Atlantic. Thus a muddy portage became the great, fortunate fact of Chicago history.

The first men, wandering south from the Bering Strait, found this crossing place to the east and south. They hunted game on the teeming prairie, raised their vast mounds across the plains all the way to the Appalachians. The great trails led to this portage. When the waters were low, cargoes were carried across the divide and canoes dragged through the mud. Wars were fought for the crossing place, though few men cared to live here. Tribes passed to eastward hunting grounds, then, a millennium later, felt the pressure of pale-faced newcomers on the seaboard. The westward retreat began.

The Algonquins, harassed by their enemies, the terrible Iroquois, knew the portage again. They called it Chicagou. In time it marked the westward limit of Iroquois power, a boundary contested fiercely by the Fox, when he was not fighting his favorite enemy, the Sioux. Here, be-

tween wars, the Illinois sometimes dwelt, until marauders from the north drove him out. The Miamis came, hunted, traded, and built villages, then yielded to the Potawatomis, themselves driven down from ancestral homes near Lake Superior.

The trails were deep, the portage well used when Jacques Cartier discovered the Gulf of St. Lawrence in 1534. Sometime during the ensuing century the first French trader heard of a great river that flowed to a southern ocean and began the search for the shortest route to the imagined wealth of China. Jean Nicolet reached Lake Michigan in 1634 and spoke of a river which left that lake to find a southern sea. Pierre d'Esprit Sieur de Radisson and his brother-in-law, Medard Chanart, sought such a route in 1654 and again in 1663. Meantime other Frenchmen were content to take the riches close at hand, trading tomahawks, guns, gunpowder, vermilion, and whisky for pelts shipped to Montreal and Quebec. And Jesuit priests built missions, pleading with the Indians not to use the guns or drink the whisky.

After 1663, when France's Louis XIV proclaimed northern America his royal province, it was decreed that a southern route must be found. In Quebec, young Louis Jolliet, explorer, geographer, and church organist, read the accounts of Father Claude Allouez, Jesuit missionary in the land of Les Reynards (the Foxes) on the western shore of Lake Michigan, then called Lake of the Illinois. Allouez wrote of "the Missipi or Great Water" which flowed south, perhaps to China. He spoke of a voyage to the Potawatomis who inhabited an area "at the foot of the Lake of the Illinois, which is called Machikiganing."

Jolliet obtained permission to search for the river. Since the Jesuits were firmly fixed along part of the route, it was considered advisable to take along a member of that order. At St. Ignace mission, opposite Mackinac, Jolliet, then twenty-eight, was joined by Jacques Marquette, a Jesuit missionary to the Hurons and a veteran of the woods. He was thirty-eight, plump, graying, and devoted to God. Jolliet and Marquette left Mackinac May 17, 1673, in two bark canoes with five French-Canadian woodsmen and Indian guides.

They reached the Mississippi by a northern route, through Wisconsin, descended to a point near the Arkansas River. Then, having determined that the Mississippi did indeed enter a southern ocean, they turned back on a voyage that was to bring the Chicago Portage into written history. It was late in the summer of 1673. "We ascended La Conception [the Mississippi] with great difficulty against the current and left it . . . to enter another river [Illinois] which took us to the Lake of the Illinois which is a much shorter way," Père Marquette reported to his superior, Father Claude Dablon. "I never saw more beautiful country than is found on this river. The prairies are covered with cattle [buffalo], stags, goats and the rivers and lakes with swans, ducks, geese, parrots and beaver. The river upon which we sailed [Illinois and Des Plaines] was wide, deep and placid for 65 leagues [305 miles] and navigable most of the year 'round. There is a portage of only half a league into the Lake of the Illinois."

The historic voyage ended at Green Bay in the fall of 1673. Jolliet wrote an enthusiastic report, urging that a canal should be dug across the portage. "A very important advantage," he said, "is that we can go easily to Florida in boats and by very good navigation. There would be needed but one canal to be made by cutting only one half a league [about two and one-half miles] of prairie to pass from the Lake of the Illinois into the St. Louis River [the Des Plaines]. The route to be taken is through Lake Erie and Lake Huron, the Lake of the Illinois, and the St. Louis River, which empties into the Mississippi, and into the Gulf of Mexico."

It was the beginning of the Chicago dream, and dream it remained for nearly two centuries. Jolliet, returning to Quebec, was caught in a struggle between Count Frontenac, the new governor, and

Chicago in 1820. This is a later copy of the first drawing ever made of the city's site by Henry R. Schoolcraft when, in that year, he arrived with Lewis Cass, governor of the Northwest Territory. Schoolcraft sketched Fort Dearborn and John Kinsey's house, on the left and right banks of the Chicago River, and predicted that an agricultural trading town would rise there. *(Chicago Historical Society.)*

the Jesuits for control of the lakes region. He was refused permission to go back. He had lost his maps and papers when his boat upset and now had to reconstruct them from memory. His enemies refused to accept these accounts as true.

Father Marquette, having reported his discoveries, was concerned now with keeping his promise to the Kaskaskia Indians to return and preach to them. On December 4, 1674, he arrived again at the Chicago Portage, found it closed by ice. Too ill to turn back, he decided to winter there, with two of his men. They built a crude hut, somewhere on the south branch of the Chicago River. During the long, cold months the ailing priest was visited by Indians, who brought him food and twelve beaver skins, and by two trappers living to the south, one Pierre Amoreau (called La Taupine, the Mole) and the other simply named "the Surgeon" in Marquette's recollections. In the spring the priest felt death was near. He turned back, leaving Chicago on March 29 to go south and east around the lake. On May 18, 1675, near the site of Ludington, Michigan, he died.

Count Frontenac, the empire builder, was eager to expand the fur trade of the West, to plant colonies there, and to break the hold of the Jesuits. He picked his man, René Robert Cavalier, Sieur de la Salle, thirty-six, an arrogant, taciturn explorer able to inspire fanatic loyalty in some men, hatred in others. La Salle, trained by the Jesuits, had quarreled with them. Indian pelts interested him more than Indian souls. In 1679 he readied *Le Griffon,* first ship of commerce on the Great Lakes, for a major expedition. He sailed to the Jesuit mission at Green Bay, where *Le Griffon* was loaded with a fortune in furs and sent back, never to be heard of again.

Ignoring Jolliet's reports on the Chicago Por-

After crossing the Chicago Portage in 1673, Louis Jolliet drew this map from memory. He urged the cutting of a canal at Chicago to link the St. Lawrence with the Gulf of Mexico. *(New York Public Library.)*

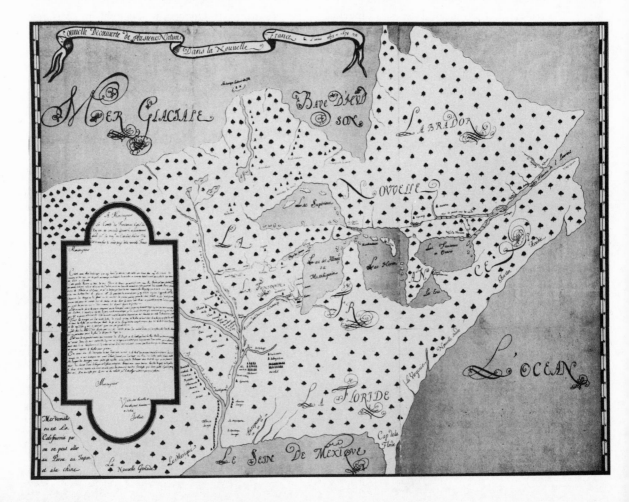

Louis Jolliet, from a bas relief in the Marquette Building, Chicago. *(Illinois State Historical Society.)*

Pere Jacques Marquette, after the painting by R. Roos in 1669. *(Chicago Historical Society.)*

Jean Baptiste Louis Franquelin, trained as an engineer, held a position as hydrographer to the king at Quebec. His great map of New France in 1684 is one of the earliest showing the Chicago Portage (Cheagoumeman). Francis Parkman believed that La Salle provided Franquelin with the information. A portion of the rare map is reproduced here. *(Chicago Antiquities.)*

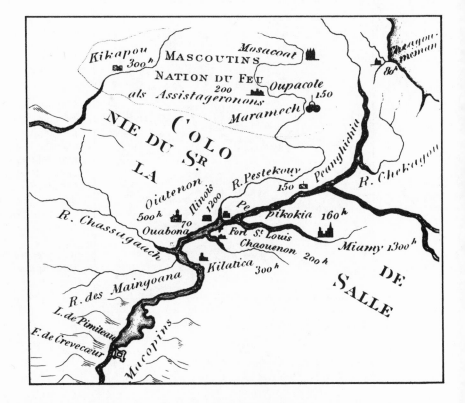

tage, La Salle led 14 men south along the east shore of Lake Michigan to the mouth of the St. Joseph River, where he built Fort Miami, named for the Indians settled there. He was joined by Henri de Tonti, a man with an iron hand and an iron will, who brought 18 men. They took canoes down the St. Joseph, portaged to the Illinois River, and built Fort Crévecoeur (Heartbreak) at Lake Peoria, called Chicago by some of the Indians.

Not until 1681 did La Salle use the Chicago Portage. In that year he began his expedition which gave France claim to Midwestern America. Tonti went ahead with a party of 23 French and 18 Indian warriors, their squaws and children. Father Zenobius Membre recorded that in December 1681 he embarked "with Sieur Henri de Tonti and part of our people on Lake Dauphin [Michigan] to go toward the Divine River, called by the Indians Checagou, in order to make necessary arrangements for our voyage. . . . The Sieur de la Salle joined us there with his troops on 4th January, 1682 and found that Tonti had had sleighs made to put all on and carry it over the Checagou, which was frozen."

La Salle perceived that this was indeed the shortest and best route South. But he was not en-chanted by it. "The basin into which you enter to go from the Lake of the Illinois to the Divine River [evidently the Des Plaines] is in no way suited for communication, there being no anchorage, wind, or entrance for a vessel," he reported to Count Frontenac. "The prairies are flooded whenever it rains . . . a channel, being dug, would fill with sand and gravel. Were this channel possible, at great expense, it would be useless, because the Divine River is not navigable for forty leagues from here to the great village of the Illinois."

La Salle, however, was of two minds about Chicago, for he wrote a letter to a friend in France predicting that someday a city would rise here. He planned a fort at the portage and, to secure his communications, induced the Miamis to sever their tenuous alliance with the Iroquois and join the Illinois, who were dominated by Fort Crévecoeur. This diplomacy exasperated Father Membre, who held the Illinois in contempt: "They are lewd, and unnaturally so, having boys dressed as women, destined for infamous purposes. They are wandering, idle, fearful, desolate, irritable, thievish, too cowardly to defend their towns, although their bowmen have great skill."

One of the earliest published maps of the Chicago Portage was prepared by William de L'Isle, royal geographer to the French king, in 1703. De L'Isle was the leading map maker of his time. The Popple map, showing a fort at Chicago in 1733, is from Henry Popple's atlas, *America Septentrionalis*, published in London. Fort Miami was actually at the mouth of the St. Joseph River, on the eastern shore of Lake Michigan, called Lake Illinois by Popple. In 1721, Father Charlevoix visited the east shore of Lake Michigan. The map at the extreme right was prepared by N. Bellin, engraver of the French Department of Marine, to illustrate the Charlevoix *History of New France* published in 1744. (Maps from *Chicago Antiquities*.)

Father Marquette's 1674 winter quarters at the Chicago Portage as imagined by Artist Lawrence C. Earle in a mural painted in 1909. *(Chicago Historical Society.)*

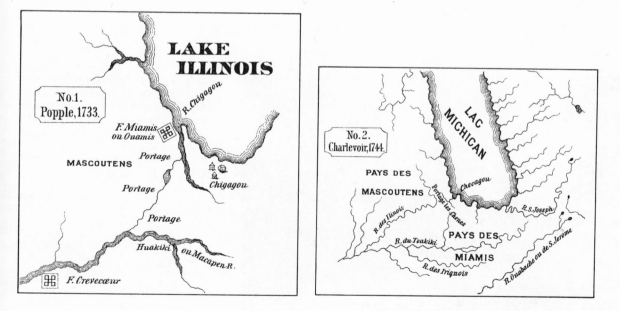

La Salle continued south, down the Mississippi. There, at its mouth, on April 9, 1682, he took possession of all lands watered by the Mississippi for King Louis, naming them Louisiana. He dispatched Tonti to strengthen Fort Crévecoeur on the Illinois, renaming it Fort St. Louis, and sent two men, André Eno and Jean Filatreau, to begin a fort at Chicago. La Salle envisioned colonies throughout this vast territory, with himself as governor of a province independent of Canada.

With money from France, La Salle planted a colony in Texas. Troubles beset him. When hardships had decimated his settlement, he started north to join Tonti, in 1687. The survivors mutinied and La Salle was slain. One of the band, Henri Joutel, led the remnants on. "We arrived at a place called Chicago, which, according to what we were told, has been so called on account of the garlic growing in this district," Joutel wrote. On April 8, 1688, Joutel and his men crossed the portage en route to Canada.

The collapse of La Salle's empire led the Jesuits and Montreal traders to take a renewed interest in Chicago, which they regarded as a gateway to the South, rather than the closed door La Salle had sought to create. The Miamis, profiting by their new alliance, established two new villages near the portage, midway between their chief towns, one on the St. Joseph River, to the east, and Maramech, on the great trail to the West. In 1696, Father Pierre Pinet set out from Mackinac to convert the Miamis at Chicago. He was joined by Father Julian Binneteau and they built the Mission of the Guardian Angel, a house of logs and bark, probably on the north branch of the river. Father Jean Francis de St. Cosme, arriving there that year en route to Cahokia, described a village of 150 huts and wigwams, and a second town of similar size nearby, to the west. The fur trade increased. It appeared that the rise of Chicago was at hand.

But that same year the French government, desiring a monopoly of the fur trade, prohibited the loose-living *coureurs de bois* from trafficking with the Indians. Only favorites of the king, with proper license, were to enjoy the profits from peltry. And in 1700, the government in Canada, still warring with the Jesuits, ordered Pinet's mission closed. The good fathers departed, sadly admitting they had made little progress among the Miamis, who were "hardened in profligacy."

For the next half-century Chicago was no-man's land. The Fox Indians to the north took to the warpath, accusing the French of selling guns

La Salle builds *Le Griffon,* first ship of commerce on the Great Lakes. Woodcut after a highly imaginative drawing by Father Louis Hennepin, published in Hennepin's *Nouvelle Decouverte,* Amsterdam, 1704. *Le Griffon* was built in 1679. *(Chicago Historical Society.)*

La Salle at Fort Frontenac, on Lake Ontario, directs the construction of boats which will be hauled across the Chicago Portage. It was on this expedition in 1682 that La Salle took possession of the Mississippi Valley for France. From a painting by Paul Strayer, Chicago artist noted for his historical scenes. Used by permission of the artist. The portrait of Henri Tonti, La Salle's lieutenant, known as the man with the iron hand, was painted from life by Nicolas Maes, a Dutch artist. *(Illinois State Historical Society.)*

to their enemies, the Sioux. In alliance with the Muscatines and Kickapoos they swept south. "May God grant that the road from Chicagwo be not closed," wrote Father Jacques Gravier at Peoria in 1701. But the Fox scattered the Miamis, the route to the Mississippi was cut. French expeditions from Detroit, St. Joseph, and Kaskaskia failed to retake the portage. In 1725, Chief Chicagou, of the Michigamea tribe, was taken to Paris by Father Nicholas Beaubois of Kaskaskia in an effort to arrange a peace. But the attempt failed. The Fox and Kickapoos were defeated in skirmishes near Chicago in 1728 and again in 1733. Still the war went on.

The French, preoccupied with the power struggle in Europe, could give only sporadic attention to the westward Indians. The unconquered Fox turned on other Indian tribes, gradually depleting their strength. In 1760, they allied themselves with their old foes, the Sioux, to attack the Kickapoos. The battle was won at terrible cost. With fewer than 300 warriors remaining, the Fox retreated to their Wisconsin homeland. The French, defeated at last in their wars with the English, secretly ceded a portion of their western lands to Spain and gave up the rest in the Treaty of Paris. The long struggle was ended, the Chicago road was again open. But now British troops would garrison the forts on the Great Lakes and the Mississippi. British law would prevail.

Settlers penned along the Atlantic coast spilled westward, finding the Ohio River a convenient route. British and American traders went into competition with the French at St. Joseph, Green Bay, St. Louis, Cahokia, and Kaskaskia. Chicago, inhabited by two Frenchmen, Sieur Jean de Liette and Jean Baptiste Guillory, remained forgotten. Chief Pontiac of the Ottawas allied the Indian tribes in a desperate effort to repel the new invaders, and lost by the Treaty of Oswego, New York, in 1766. The Potawatomis, who had been at Chicago in the time of Allouez, now returned and laid claim to most of northern Illinois. They were indolent, but friendly, welcoming the few French traders who appeared, married into their tribe, and settled with them. Sleepy Chicago was beyond civilization, undisturbed by the little British navy which plied the Great Lakes. British officers who proposed a fort at Chicago were ignored by the government in London.

With the outbreak of the Revolutionary War, the western settlers feared that England would rally the Indians to attack on the undefended flank. In Kentucky, George Rogers Clark, twenty-six-year-old agent of the Ohio Company, called for preventive war in the West. He organized a Kentucky militia, had himself elected major, and persuaded his neighbors to send him to Virginia for help. The House of Burgesses promised money and powder, plus 300 acres of land, for every man who would join Clark's expedition against the British. They created the County of Kentucky for the government of the western area, and authorized Clark to march. With only 175 men, he moved on Fort Kaskaskia and Cahokia, in Illinois. These places, largely French despite their English garrisons, surrendered quickly to Clark's "Long Knives," who arrived under the rattlesnake flag of Virginia. Kaskaskia fell on July 4, 1778, and in December the Virginia assembly created the County of Illinois, appointing John Todd, twenty-eight, county lieutenant, or governor. The arrangement took no notice of a place called Chicago.

General Henry Hamilton, "the hair buyer," countered Clark's thrust by reinforcing Fort Vincennes on the Ohio, a move intended to cut off the American forces. But on February 5, 1779, Clark began his heroic march across the drowned lands. He arrived before Vincennes February 23, deployed his men to give the effect of a great army, and on the twenty-fifth called for Hamilton's unconditional surrender. The British capitulated. The West was won for the colonies.

By the treaty of 1783, England yielded all of the territory east of the Mississippi. Since Spain held the Mississippi and the fur trade was conducted at a loss, considering the cost of forts and garrisons to maintain it, Lord Shellbourne, conducting negotiations for England, did not think the West worth keeping. But British traders declined to leave and the garrison at Detroit stayed on, protecting the trade with Canada.

Gen. Henry Hamilton, British commander, and his garrison of 79 officers and men formally turn over Fort Sackville at Vincennes to George Rogers Clark, February 25, 1779. From a painting by Gary Sheahan. Used by permission of the artist.

The Indian Treaty of Grenville, 1795, in which the United States acquired title to land at Chicago. This scene, believed to have been painted by one of the officers present, purports to show General "Mad Anthony" Wayne (front view with epaulets) listening to Chief Little Turtle of the Miamis, with William Henry Harrison (hat in hand) between the two. The officer kneeling is Captain William Wells, who acted as interpreter and transcribed Little Turtle's speech. *(Chicago Historical Society.)*

Chicago's future seemed bleak. The fur trading post at the portage was cut off on the south by the Spaniards at New Orleans, on the north by the British. With three powers grasping at the midcontinental lifeline, its commerce stagnated. The fur trade at Chicago waned to nearly nothing.

Passage of the Northwest Ordinance in April 1787 spurred the settlement of lands in Ohio, Indiana, Michigan, and southern Illinois. A government was organized for the vast territory, setting up conditions for ultimate statehood on a basis of equality with the original thirteen. Schools would be forever encouraged in the new territory, free worship would be guaranteed. Article 6 provided that "There shall be neither slavery nor involuntary servitude in the said territory other than as a punishment for crimes." Territorial lines were drawn for an area bounded by the Mississippi, Ohio, and Wabash rivers and thence north to the boundary with Canada. Congress agreed to create states "north of an east and west line through the southerly bend or extremity of Lake Michigan" whenever any such region should organize a government and have 60,000 free inhabitants and petition for admission to the Union.

Land companies were organized to exploit the rich possibilities of the Old Northwest. Settlements sprang up along the rivers, lands were cleared, towns planted, roads built. The newcomers had no urge to trade with Indians. As the settlements marched west, forests disappeared, hunting vanished, and a traffic in corn and grain flowed east, along the Ohio and its tributary rivers. The Indians rallied for war, under Tecumseh, the Shawnee chief. They were met and defeated by the forces of General "Mad Anthony" Wayne at the Battle of Fallen Timbers. In the subsequent Treaty of Greenville, which General Wayne imposed on August 4, 1795, the Indians ceded land for three forts, one at Peoria, one at the mouth of the Illinois River, the third at Chicago. This realestate transaction, most momentous for Chicago, was simply stated:

"One piece of Land Six Miles Square at the mouth of the Chickago River emptying into the southwest end of Lake Michigan where a fort formerly stood."

Fort Dearborn and the Massacre

In 1796, British troops at last prepared to quit the lake country under a new treaty with England obtained by John Jay. At the same time, the Spaniards agreed to open the Mississippi to American trade. On July 11, 1796, United States troops took possession of Detroit. There was talk of a series of forts, including one at Chicago. But first a Great Lakes fleet would be needed for reinforcement and supply. Construction of two ships was ordered. The brig *Adams* and the sloop *Tracy* were put on the ways in a new shipyard at Detroit.

Nothing happened at Chicago. In August 1798, William Burnett, a trader settled in St. Joseph, informed his Montreal supplier that he had taken a house near the Chicago Portage in anticipation of the arrival of a garrison in the fall. He expected to require "a good deal of liquors and supplies." No garrison appeared, Spain again closed the Mississippi mouth, and Burnett remained in St. Joseph.

The trade at Chicago, meanwhile, was in the capable hands of Jean Baptiste Point du Sable, a dusky man of mystery who had dwelt in ducal style on the north bank of the river, near the lake, since 1784. He had previously lived in St. Joseph, where in 1779 British soldiers arrested him on suspicion of trading with the enemy and took him to Mackinac. Du Sable's knowledge of Indian affairs had so impressed the British governor, Patrick Sinclair, that the trader was put to managing Sinclair's fur post, The Pinery, on the St. Clair River.

Three years later, Du Sable turned up in Chicago, where he built a 22-by-40 foot house of logs and bark and filled it with paintings and fine furniture. In Detroit, where Du Sable bought supplies, it was said that he was the son of a Frenchman and a Negro mother. Du Sable himself sometimes said he was from Santo Domingo, and at other times he claimed to be a Potawatomi chief. He married a Potawatomi woman, Catherine, and prospered in the fur trade. Within ten years his improvement consisted of two barns, a horse mill, a bakehouse, a workshop, a dairy, a poultry house, and a smokehouse. His inventory included two mules, 30 head of cattle, 20 hogs, and a large store of tools.

In 1796, Du Sable had been joined by Antoine Ouilmette, a wizened French-Indian almost as dark as Du Sable himself, who settled his Potawatomi wife, Archange, and their brood of children in a log cabin to the west. Ouilmette aided Du Sable in the fur trade but was chiefly occupied in hauling boats and supplies across the Chicago Portage.

With talk rife of a fort to be built at Chicago, Du Sable inexplicably sold his house and possessions to Jean la Lime, another St. Joseph trader. He then disappeared into southern Illinois, and eventually died heavily in debt.

In 1800, Spain ceded its Mississippi River properties back to France. In 1803, the United States began negotiations with France which culminated in the Louisiana Purchase. Early that same year the government moved to claim its Chicago land. On March 9, General Henry Dearborn, Secretary of War, ordered the dispatch of an officer and six men from Detroit to select a site for a fort at Chicago. Six weeks later, Captain John Whistler was chosen to build and command the new outpost. Whistler, a burly man six feet two inches tall, was an experienced officer who had commanded Fort Howard at Green Bay. The father of 15 children, he found it impossible to support his family on his $40.00 a month pay and was incessantly harassed by creditors. They were reluctant to have him disappear into the wilderness, but, after some legal difficulties, Whistler left Detroit to survey the route to Chicago. On July 14 he was back to start the first troops, under Lieutenant James Strode Swearingen, on their march. Captain Whistler put his large family aboard the supply ship *Tracy,* arranging to rendezvous with Swearingen at St. Joseph.

The troops reached the John Kinzie improvement on the St. Joseph River on July 25, and three days later they encamped on the east shore of Lake Michigan, awaiting the *Tracy,* which arrived August 12. Canoes and bateaux were obtained, and on August 16 the march resumed. The troops proceeded on the beach around the lake, and the supplies, women, and children crossed by boat.

Early on August 17, 1803, the army of blue-coated men in pigtails reached the Potawatomi camp on the Calumet River. Indians peered from the sand dunes along the line of march, but there was no show of hostility. At 2 P.M. that broiling August day Lieutenant Swearingen topped the sand dunes near the river and saw Chicago. It was a depressing sight. Beyond the dunes, the prairie lay like a great saucer, with Mud Lake steaming in the center of it and tiny creeks cutting through the marshlands down to the river, which curved lazily along the lake front. Beyond the bend of the river, some 200 yards from the lake shore, squatted a few cabins and barns. Opposite, on comparatively high ground, eight feet above the water, was the fort site chosen by Captain Whistler. The river, Swearingen noted, was about 30 yards wide, and, although it was said to be 18 feet deep, the water lay foul and dead.

When the *Tracy* arrived, standing outside the sand bar which closed the mouth of the river, hundreds of Indians appeared among the dunes. They were curious and friendly, watching in awe as supplies were lightered from the ship. Captain Whistler at once put the men to work pitching tents for the temporary camp and took over La Lime's

Fort Dearborn in 1804, from the Chicago River. A mural by Lawrence C. Earle in 1909. *(Chicago Historical Society.)*

house for his family. The next day sawyers were sent out to the wooded rises in the sea of marshland to fell trees for the stockade. Since there was a shortage of horses and oxen, men dragged logs to the building site. The Potawatomis, weary of watching in the extreme heat, withdrew to their camps. Whistler learned from La Lime that they could muster 1,000 warriors, and their allies, the Kickapoos, 500 more. Whistler had 66 soldiers in his command. He pressed the building of the stockade.

Yet work on Fort Dearborn proceeded slowly. There was a lack of saws and sawyers to finish the oak logs, corn for the oxen, clothing for the men. The garrison boasted two fifers, but no fife. Fortunately the winter was mild and the hunting was good. The men added fowl, venison, and bear meat to their meager rations. But in the summer of 1804 the fort was still incomplete, the supply problem unsolved.

Whistler got unexpected help from a new arrival. A fast-talking, hot-tempered Scotsman, he was John Kinzie, a St. Joseph trader who had bought La Lime's house and now trebled Chicago's civilian population by moving in his family and retainers. Kinzie was born in Quebec, December 27, 1763, the son of a Scotch military surgeon. He had been in the fur trade since boyhood, first along the Maumee River in Ohio until he was driven out by General Wayne, then at St. Joseph. He now claimed American citizenship, but his enemies asserted that he was a British

The building of Fort Dearborn in the summer of 1803. Captain Whistler (with glass) and his engineer, Lieutenant Swearingen. Offshore, the sloop, *Tracy*. Lack of horses and oxen forced men to drag logs to the site. A painting by Paul Strayer, reproduced by permission of the artist.

agent. He was unquestionably able in the arts of dealing with Indians and procuring supplies, and Captain Whistler eagerly solicited his aid. Soon supplies were moving down from Detroit in huge bateaux and Mackinac boats, plied by French-Canadians and half-breeds whose French boat songs could be heard a mile away. Such boats could cross the Chicago sand bar without trouble. They discharged their cargoes and some proceeded over the portage to Peoria, where Kinzie was in partnership with Thomas Forsythe and fur packs awaited them. Soon Kinzie had trading posts along the Rock River and near Milwaukee. He enlarged his house, built a porch across the front, and added to his staff of servants and engagees. By the time the fort was finished, Kinzie had made it clear that he was the top civilian in the town.

The fort, said William Johnson, a visitor, was "the neatest and best garrison in the country." Captain Whistler built it from his own plans. Inside a 12-foot stockade, surmounted with iron crow's-feet, were two blockhouses, one with two cannon, the other with one cannon and a large stand of small arms. The main gate faced south, flanked by soldiers' barracks and the hospital. To the east and west, against an inner palisade, were the officers' barracks, including the commandant's quarters. To the north of the parade was the stone magazine, the contractor's store, and a storehouse. A covered way, in which a well was dug, led to the river.

Two log houses south of the fort, beyond the garrison gardens, were occupied by Matthew Irwin, the government contractor, and Charles Jouett, the Indian agent. Both houses had loopholes for defense. To the west lay the fort cemetery. About three miles southwest, along the south branch of the river, was the farm of Charles Lee, who supplied butter and eggs to the fort. John K. Clark, a cattle dealer, built a house and corral at the south fork of the river. On the north, the homes of Kinzie, Ouilmette, La Lime, now interpreter to the garrison; Thomas Burns, a soldier whose enlistment had run out; and a French half-breed, Pierre Le May, completed the roster of villagers.

Life was not unpleasant at the fort. By day it hummed as the men of the First Infantry drilled, mounted guard, maintained their gear. Indian chiefs arrived and departed, white visitors were welcomed, ships lying beyond the bar discharged supplies for the troops and government factory. In summer, the soldiers worked in the gardens, swam in the river east of the fort. There were fiesta days, as when William Whistler, son of the commandant, challenged the Indian runners to a five-mile race and won it, before throngs of howling savages and whooping soldiers. There were hunting forays, wrestling matches, dances at the Kinzie home when the officers would permit it and John was there to play the fiddle.

Beyond the walls, Indian tribes encamped as they arrived with furs and complaints. Pigs and half-breed children wallowed in the mudholes, drovers brought their cattle down to Clark's, and now and then a wagon train arrived from Detroit or Fort Wayne. By night, when the Indians had been paid, drunken braves rampaged, soldiers sought out squaws, fights broke out, thieves raided cattle pens, gardens, and piggeries. Chiefs protested that their warriors were debauched by the liquor trade. Braves were known to kill their wives and fling children into campfires, and squaws, liking whisky no less, sold their favors to any comer for a gill of spirits. The traders with their Potawatomi wives accepted the changes philosophically. They sold their services to the fort, rum to their brothers-in-law, and remained on excellent terms with both.

The struggle for the liquor business embroiled the officers and civilians in a vicious feud. Dr. John Cooper, the fort surgeon, had obtained sutlers' privileges and was heavily engaged in selling rum to the redskins. So was Matthew Irwin, whose dealings aroused the Potawatomis to demonstrate in protest. Cooper and Irwin allied themselves against Kinzie, who enjoyed the confidence of the Indians, paid them in silver when they wished it, and generally dominated the trade of the area. Kinzie also sold liquor, and when Captain Whistler backed Dr. Cooper, Kinzie swiftly joined forces with Irwin. They accused Whistler of using soldier labor for his personal gain and sought to have him court-martialed. Lieutenant Thomas

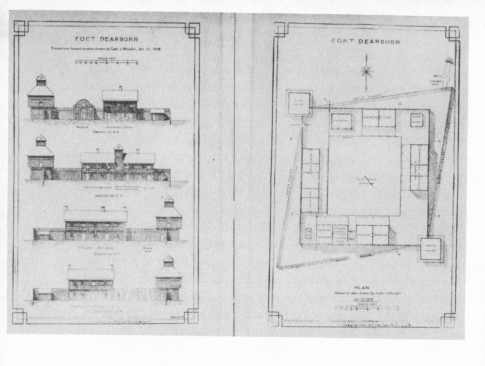

Left. The plan and elevations of Fort Dearborn redrawn by George H. Fergus in 1897 from Captain John Whistler's plans submitted to the war department in 1808. *Below.* Inside the fort looking toward the powder magazine, with the contractor's store on the right. These restorations for A Century of Progress Exposition were based on Whistler's plans. *(Chicago Historical Society.)*

The Fort Dearborn restoration from the west (top), showing the palisade, the northwest blockhouse, stone powder magazine, and the officers' barracks. Below, interior of the restored fort, across the parade ground. Fire destroyed the restoration in 1939. *(Kaufmann-Fabry.)*

A view of Fort Dearborn, based on Whistler's plans, drawn by Charles H. Ourand in 1897. The gates opened on what is now Michigan Avenue. *(Chicago Historical Society.)*

Hamilton, Whistler's son-in-law, challenged Kinzie to a duel but the trader cursed him roundly and declined.

The affair became so odious that the Secretary of War ordered all of the officers scattered. Whistler himself returned to Detroit. Kinzie promptly began feuding with Irwin and La Lime, the interpreter. Kinzie's supporters said that he wanted a fair deal for the Indians, a view the Potawatomis seemed to share. His enemies insisted that he wanted a monopoly of the rum trade.

The arrival of Captain Nathan Heald to command Fort Dearborn failed to check the strife. Heald, New Hampshire born, had formerly commanded at Fort Wayne. A careful, methodical officer, he sought to give his attention to the fort. But he was soon involved in a struggle with Kinzie, despite the fact that one of his officers, Lieutenant Linai T. Helm, had married Kinzie's stepdaughter, Margaret, a pretty girl of eighteen. In April 1812, the feud flared into a knife fight that proved fatal for La Lime. Kinzie, claiming he fought in self-defense, fled to the shelter of his Indian friends in Wisconsin. Irwin left Fort

Dearborn for Detroit, county seat of the territory, where he charged that La Lime had been murdered.

Other troubles beset the fort. English traders were suspected of having aroused the Indians. "They labor by every unprincipled means to instigate the savages against Americans, to inculcate the idea that we intend to drive the Indians beyond the Mississippi, and that in every purchase of land the government defrauds them," complained Dr. Isaac Van Voorhis, new surgeon at the fort.

The English were indeed busy. They distributed arms and gifts, welcomed Tecumseh to their side and made him a general. Robert Dickson, British trader, organized a company of warriors for an attack on Mackinac if war should come. In April, Captain Heald put Fort Dearborn in a virtual state of siege after Winnebagos invaded the Lee farm at Hardscrabble and scalped two men. Down to 56 regulars in his garrison, he organized the 15 civilian men at Chicago into a militia and forbade the Indians to approach the fort.

Kinzie, deep in Indian country, sent a letter to Heald, informing him that an attack on Mackinac

56

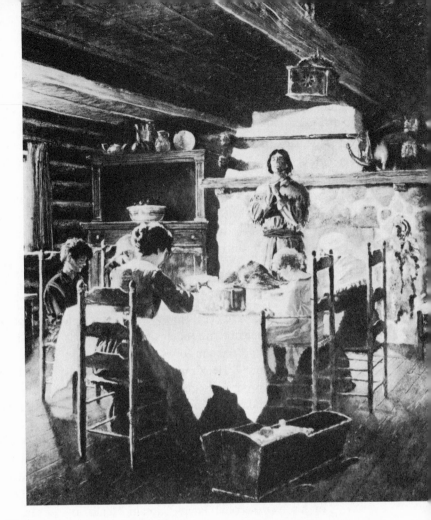

A Chicago family in 1808 as depicted by Paul
Strayer from relics and accounts of pioneers. Used
by permission of the artist. Below, at left, John
Kinzie. At right, Alexander Robinson, Potawatomi chief who helped to rescue the Kinzies from
the massacre. *(Chicago Historical Society.)*

was imminent. If it succeeded, Kinzie warned, Fort Dearborn would be next. On July 18, a month to the day after the declaration of war, British troops joined Dickson's Indians before Mackinac and the fort was surrendered without a shot being fired. The news spread. More tribes took to the warpath. Settlers fled to the forts. Kinzie returned to Chicago, moved his family and retainers inside the stockade, and set himself up as an unwelcome advisor to Heald.

On August 9, an Indian runner delivered General William Hull's order to evacuate. Heald was directed to join Hull at Detroit, or to retreat to Fort Wayne, whichever seemed safer, and to dispose of the government stores as he thought proper. "The neighboring Indians got the news as early as I did and came in to receive the goods in the factory store," Heald wrote later. Hull followed up his order by requesting Captain James Rhea, commandant at Fort Wayne, to send assistance to Fort Dearborn. Captain William Wells, veteran Indian fighter and Heald's old friend, started for Chicago at once, with Corporal Walter Jordan and 27 Miami warriors. He arrived on August 13, to find great indecision at the fort.

In his own account later, Captain Heald asserted that he wished to give a part of his supplies to the Indians, and to destroy the guns, ammunition, and liquor, "fearing they would make bad use of this if put in their possession." Lieutenant Helm, son-in-law of Kinzie, claimed it was Kinzie who wanted the arms and liquor destroyed and that he, Kinzie, and Wells jointly called upon Heald to take such action. Heald, according to Helm, consented to act only when Kinzie forged an order from General Hull, calling for destruction of the guns, powder, and liquor. Later, such an order was found, but not in Hull's handwriting. Heald himself said that disposition of government property was left to his discretion.

Shortly before the arrival of Captain Wells, Captain Heald had distributed much trade goods to the Potawatomis, in exchange for a promise of safe conduct. That night the whisky and guns were dumped in the well and the river. On August 14, Black Partridge, a friendly Potawatomi chief, called on Captain Heald to warn that he could not restrain his young men, who had learned of the destruction of guns and liquor. He returned his medal, a gift from the government.

Wells and Kinzie were now sure that the Indians would attack. Captain Heald still hoped for safe conduct, but insisted that he must, in any event, carry out his orders. Kinzie made his own

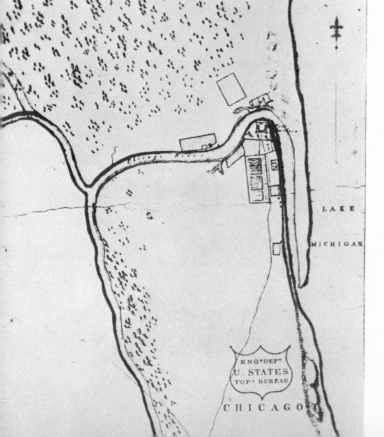

An 1808 map, showing the fort and the Chicago River turning south to what is now Madison Street. (*Chicago Public Library*.)

Above. The town's first permanent residence, Point du Sable's house opposite the fort, later owned by John Kinzie, who added the porch. At left, Antoine Ouilmette's log house. *(Chicago Historical Society.)*

Below. Painting by F. R. Glass shows Black Partridge returning his medal to Captain Nathan Heald, Fort Dearborn commandant, on the eve of the massacre. Lieutenant Helm, standing; Captain Wells at extreme left. "I will not wear a token of peace while I am compelled to act as an enemy," said the chief, according to Helm. *(Chicago Public Library.)*

Left. Carl Rohl-Smith's sculpture of Margaret Helm's rescue by Black Partridge as Ensign George Ronan, slain in the fighting, lies at her feet. "A young Indian raised a tomahawk over me," Mrs. Helm recalled. "I avoided the blow . . . exerting my utmost strength to get his scalping knife. I was dragged from his grasp by another and older Indian . . ." *(Chicago Historical Society.)*

Below. Mrs. Heald defends herself in the fight at the wagons. She was wounded, but recovered following her rescue by Chandonnai, a half-breed, and Alexander Robinson. From an old engraving. *(Chicago Public Library.)*

preparations for escape, arranging with Indian friends to have a boat ready on the river. He agreed to march with the troops, however, to help protect his stepdaughter, the young wife of Lieutenant Helm, who insisted on accompanying her husband.

On the night of August 14 preparations for the march were completed. Soldiers and militiamen each received twenty-five rounds of ammunition, supply wagons were loaded, women and their children were assigned their places in the line of march. Two of the mothers had babes in arms, a third, the wife of Fielding Corbin, was awaiting the birth of her third child.

The morning of August 15 came clear and hot. At nine o'clock the stockade gates swung open. Commands were shouted. Riders clattered into formation, the wagons creaked. The fifers sounded the mournful tones of the "Dead March" from Handel's *Saul*. Captain Wells, riding out with 15 of his Miamis, had blackened his face, the Indian sign of disaster. Behind them the garrison marched out in order, led by Captain Heald and Lieutenant Helm. They were followed by the women and children, some riding in the two baggage wagons, guarded by Dr. Van Voorhis and Ensign George Ronan. At the rear were 12 members of the militia, Kinzie, unarmed, and 12 Miami warriors, mounted.

A few of the promised Potawatomi escort appeared as the garrison left the fort and proceeded east toward the river. But as the troops turned south, the escort disappeared behind the sand dunes. It was oppressively hot and still.

About a mile and a half from the fort, Captain Wells saw Indians lurking in the hills, their heads popping up like turtles. He sped back toward Heald, signaling that they were surrounded. Heald ordered his garrison troops to charge the dunes. The Indians began a heavy fire, falling back as the soldiers topped the ridges. Musket fire cracked on all sides. Captain Heald and his men were cut off from the wagon train. The Miami warriors deserted, thundering off down the beach. Lieutenant Helm ordered his men to reload and found he was cut off from Captain Heald. He had 27 men, many

wounded, and he estimated the Indians surrounding him at 300.

Now the fury of the attack was directed at the wagons. Here the militia fought hand to hand, until all were slaughtered. Van Voorhis and Ronan fell, and crazed warriors turned upon the women and children. The women fought with knives and swords. They were swiftly overwhelmed. Infuriated savages swarmed into the wagons, splitting the skulls of the children and hacking to bits the bodies of Mrs. Corbin and Cicely, Mrs. Heald's slave girl.

As the attack on the wagons began, Captain Wells rode shouting through the hail of musket fire in an attempt to break the Indians' charge. Both the captain and his horse were hit by musket balls and they fell, the horse pinning his rider. Wells fired again at his foe then, seeing a warrior take aim, he yelled insults until the shot drove home. A brave named Pee-so-tum took his scalp, another cut out his heart, and the two divided and ate it, hoping thus to acquire his courage. Later his head was mounted on a pole and paraded along the Indian lines.

Nearby, at the wagons, another brave man died, Sergeant Otho Hayes. His gun empty, he rammed his bayonet into the chest of a savage attacking with a tomahawk. The hatchet clove his skull and they fell together.

Captain Heald and those of his troops that survived finally joined Lieutenant Helm on a slight rise where the Indians hesitated to follow. They sent Pierre le Claire, a half-breed employee of Kinzie, and Blackbird, one of the chiefs, to demand a surrender. Heald promised to pay $100 for each life spared. The soldiers at first were disposed to fight, but Heald made it an order. They dropped their guns. Indians surrounded them and marched them up the beach.

They were struck with horror at the slaughter. Maddened warriors still were scalping victims, dispatching wounded. Mutilated bodies were strewn across the beach. The unborn child of Mrs. Corbin had been torn from the body of its mother and decapitated. Helm saw a headless woman he thought was his wife. She was Mrs. Corbin. A squaw, armed with a stable fork, was stabbing it into the body of Thomas Burns, wounded in the fight at the wagons; she continued to torture him until he died.

Of all the men at the wagons, only John Kinzie escaped. The Potawatomis were credited with saving him. According to Corporal Jordan, himself saved by a friendly Confute chief, only Kickapoos and Winnebagos, 600 of them, were in the fight. In the confusion, the Potawatomis, To-pee-nee-bee, Black Partridge, and Chee-chee-bing-way (Alexander Robinson) succeeded in rescuing Kinzie, Mrs. Helm, and Mrs. Heald, badly wounded. They guided them to a boat where Mrs. Kinzie, four of her children, and some servants had been waiting, and crossed to the Kinzie house.

There Kinzie removed shot from Mrs. Heald's arms while friendly Indians stood guard.

That night the Indians fired the fort. As flames lighted the sky, the warriors danced and howled and squaws tormented the wounded prisoners. The day at last ended. In ten minutes of action that morning, 26 of the 55 soldiers had been slain, all 12 of the militia died, and two women and 12 children were brutally murdered. Of 95 who marched from the fort that morning, not including the Miamis, only 43 were left alive.

Three days later, as the Kinzies and Mrs. Helm and Mrs. Heald were taken to St. Joseph, only the powder magazine remained standing at the fort. To the south, mutilated bodies lay unburied in the sun.

The fight at the wagons, in which the women and children were slain, is depicted by Ralph Fletcher Seymour, artist, author, and publisher who has specialized in Chicago lore. The Fort Dearborn massacre took place near what is now Eighteenth Street and Calumet Avenue. Used by permission of the artist.

Canal and Boom Town

IV

Again Chicago was a wilderness. The war ended with the Peace of Ghent in 1814 but it was June 1816 before Captain Hezekiah Bradley and 112 men were dispatched by boat from Detroit to rebuild Fort Dearborn. The bones of the massacre victims were buried, trees along the north shore were cut and rafted to the site, and a new stronghold arose. John Kinzie and his family returned to their home. Irwin, the government contractor, had insisted in Washington that John Kinzie instigated the Fort Dearborn massacre in order to destroy all witnesses to the slaying of La Lime, but this wild charge was ignored and Kinzie became official interpreter to the garrison.

A fierce competition for the diminishing fur trade began. John Jacob Astor, seeking to build a monopoly for his American Fur Company, sent Jean Baptiste Beaubien from Milwaukee to Chicago as his agent. Beaubien took over the government house on the lake shore south of the fort, settled his Indian wife and 13 children there, and proceeded to outtrade Kinzie and John Crafts, also from Milwaukee. Crafts soon gave up and sold out to Beaubien. Young Jacob Varnum, the new factor, brought his bride to the 20-by-20-foot log house that served as his store and home. He was well supplied with the usual trade goods—arm bands, blankets, blue cloth, wampum, thread, needles, gorgets, gunpowder, kettles, earbobs, mirrors, snuff, stirrup irons, tomahawks, tobacco, pipes, vermilion, scalping knives, shoes, scarlet cloth, and, of course, whisky and rum. But he found the Indian trade to be dying. "That summer," he wrote, "we had little else to do than fight mosquitoes."

By the winter of 1819, trade and social life perked up. "Several of the officers brought on their families and all seem disposed to be social and friendly," Varnum noted. "We have evening parties, with dancing and amusements." One of the newcomers was Gurdon S. Hubbard, a strapping sixteen-year-old apprentice to Astor's fur company, who had walked into Chicago the year before. Hubbard stayed, but most visitors moved on, seeking farm lands to the west, or the lead mines at Galena.

In 1820, General Lewis Cass, governor of Michigan Territory, arrived on an inspection tour. His mineralogist, Henry R. Schoolcraft, wrote a glowing report:

The country around Chicago is the most fertile and beautiful that can be imagined. . . . It is already the seat of several flourishing plantations and [should] become one of the most attractive fields for the immigrant. To the ordinary advantages of an agricultural marketing town, it must, hereafter, add that of a depot, for inland commerce, between the northern and southern sections of the Union, and a great throughfare for strangers, merchants and travelers.

Cass and Schoolcraft urged the construction of a canal through the portage, a project of prime interest to the Chicagoans. Three years later, as there was talk that Fort Dearborn might be abandoned, Major Stephen H. Long arrived on a government survey. He agreed that a canal could be built, but his mineralogist, Prof. William H. Keating, wrote a blistering report on the town's prospects:

The new fort and lighthouse as seen from the west by Francis de Castelnau, who visited Chicago in 1838. From his *Vues et Souvenirs de L'Amerique du Nord,* published in Paris, 1842. *(Chicago Historical Society.)*

Early Chicago centered around Wolf Point, at the juncture of the north and south branches of the river. At left, Wolf Tavern, erected by James Kinzie and Archibald Caldwell in 1829. Opposite Samuel Miller built his log and deal inn a year later. Nearby Alexander Robinson kept an Indian store and tavern. The above sketch first appeared in the *Chicago Magazine* in 1857, purportedly from a drawing by George Davis, made on the site, in 1834. *(Newberry Library.)*

Mark Beaubien, twenty-six, erected his log tavern on a lot purchased from James Kinzie in 1828. When Chicago was plotted, it developed that Beaubien's house was in the middle of Lake Street. Mark moved to the corner of Lake and Market streets, added a two-story frame structure, and became famous as the fiddle-playing host of the Sauganash Hotel, named for Billy Caldwell, the Potawatomi chief. *(Chicago Public Library.)*

We are greatly disappointed. Fertile soil? The garrison of 70 to 90 men cannot subsist on the grain raised in this country! The village . . . consists of a few huts, inhabited by a miserable race of men, scarcely equal to the Indians from whom they are descended. Their log or bark houses are low, filthy, disgusting. As a place of business it offers no inducement to the settler, for the whole annual amount of trade on the lake did not exceed a cargo of five or six schooners.

Keating allowed that when the valleys of the Illinois and Des Plaines became populated, Chicago might become a busier place, but he added crushingly:

The communication will be limited, the dangers of navigation on the lake, the scarcity of harbors, must ever prove a serious obstacle to the increase of the commercial importance of Chicago. Indeed, when the game is gone, it is doubtful that even the Indians will reside here much longer.

So, having established themselves among the most inaccurate prophets in history, Long and Keating hired guides to conduct them through the wilderness to Fort Winnebago, and continued their tour.

Keating's views aroused the supporters of the canal. It was a project on which northwestern politicians and many others were agreed. Albert Gallatin, Secretary of the Treasury, had urged such a canal in 1807. John C. Calhoun, Secretary of War, had backed it as a defense measure in 1819. When Illinois had been admitted as a state in 1818, the territorial representative, Nathaniel Pope, had induced Congress to move the boundaries of Illinois from the tip of Lake Michigan forty-one miles north to insure that an eventual canal would provide access to Illinois from a Lake Michigan port. Otherwise, Pope pointed out, the South would settle and control the new state.

With political as well as economic issues involved, the North and Northwest pressed Congress with demands that Chicago harbor improvement and canal construction start at once. Governor Cass drafted a passionate sixteen-page letter to Calhoun. Admitting that Chicago had only four families, Cass declared that development of the town would lead to the settlement of 15,000,000 acres of government land. "I consider the post at Chicago more important than at Green Bay," he wrote. "Its evacuation will give a death blow to all hopes of settling that part of Illinois." Calhoun, a southerner, now opposed the canal, but Daniel P. Cook, the new Illinois congressman, was able to rally northern support and obtained a grant of 224,333 acres of land along a strip ten miles wide from Chicago to La Salle, the alternate sections to be sold to finance the canal. A canal commission was authorized to plot two towns, one at Chicago, one at Ottawa, and to proceed with the sale of land. Surveyor James Thompson laid out Chicago in section 9, extending from Madison Street north to Kinzie, beyond the river, and State Street west to Des Plaines, 48 blocks and fractional blocks. The survey was completed and the plot filed for record August 4, 1830.

Now, Chicago was legally in existence.

There was no rush for bargains when the land was offered at auction in September. Residents who were little more than squatters had no choice but to buy a legal title at prices averaging $35.00 a lot. Jean Beaubien, occupying a choice acreage south of the fort, refused to pay a cent, asserting the land was already his. Nor did the land to the west, along State Street, interest him. He knew well enough that it was under water half the year when he crossed that way by boat to visit his brother, Mark. Only 26 lots were sold, plus two 80-acre tracts outside the town, the latter bringing $80.00 each. Robert Kinzie, son of John who had died in 1828, traveled to Palestine in southern Illinois to register his title to 102 acres on the north side of the river but he did not bother to claim 55 acres immediately to the west. "We've got enough," he told his mother.

With the completion of the Erie Canal, settlers were heading west, but not to Chicago. Buffalo, Toledo, Cincinnati, and St. Louis became flourishing towns. Even Michigan City, across the lake from Chicago, had a population of 3,000. Galena rivaled Nauvoo and Shawneetown as Illinois' chief cities. John Noble, arriving from St. Louis in 1830, could not even find Chicago. "I hit the woods to the northeast," he told friends later. "Then I wandered down upon a half-dozen log houses and asked about Chicago. 'You're in it, stranger,' they told me."

The town, such as it was, clustered around the forks of the river, a half mile west of the fort. In 1829, James Kinzie and Archibald Caldwell put up a log hotel on the west branch. For a time Elijah Wentworth took over the Kinzie-Caldwell inn. It was called "Old Geese" in compliment to Wentworth's favorite expression until he killed a wolf in his meat house, when the name Wolf Tavern was applied and stuck. Across the river to the east Samuel Miller built an inn of logs and clapboard. To the south, J. W. Titus and Patrick Murphy opened a hostelry they proudly and aptly called "The Rat Castle."

But the famous tavern of the time was Mark Beaubien's Sauganash. Mark arrived from Detroit in 1826 to visit his brother Jean, stayed on to convert a log house just south of the river, opposite Miller's, into a hotel. It was a grubby hole, filled with rats, drunken brawlers, and grumpy Indians. Mark, like the others, charged prices imposed by the county officials at Peoria: 25 cents for a half pint of wine, rum, or brandy; one shilling (12½ cents) for a half pint of whisky, 25 cents for breakfast, dinner or supper, and 37½ cents for keeping and feeding a horse for twenty-four hours. But Mark was a man of charm, who could lure unwary strangers to his establishment and somehow keep them. He acquired a ferry to facilitate

They brought the canal to Chicago. Governor Lewis Cass (left); Congressman Nathaniel Pope (center); who gained the Chicago area for Illinois; and Congressman Daniel P. Cook (right); for whom Cook County is named. (*Chicago Public Library.*)

Interior of the new Fort Dearborn as sketched by W. E.
S. Trowbridge. *(Chicago Historical Society.)*

Mark Beaubien (left), opened his Sauganash Tavern after he arrived from
Detroit to visit his brother, Jean (right) the rich fur trader. Gurdon S. Hubbard
(center) shortly after he walked into town to buy furs. *(Chicago Public Library.)*

South Water Street in 1833, looking east from the school built by John Stephen Wright, taught by Elizabeth Chappel. *(Chicago Historical Society.)*

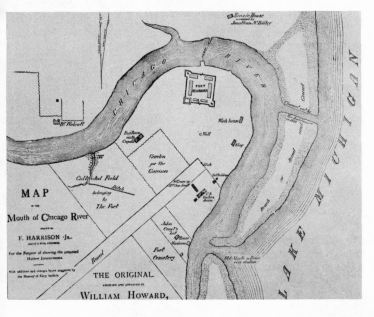

Right. James Thompson's plat of Chicago in 1830. *(Illinois Central.) Above.* Early map of Chicago, showing channel dug through sand bar in 1828 by soldiers from Fort Dearborn. *(Chicago Historical Society.)*

South Water Street in 1834, looking west from Wright's school toward the new Dearborn Street drawbridge at the right. *(Chicago Historical Society.)*

his theft of customers from his competitors across the river. What his inn lacked in comfort, Mark made up in affability. He sang, played the fiddle, and laughed infectiously when guests complained. By 1835 he had quadrupled the size of his inn, and in boom times packed 50 men into his loft at night. Some guests swore that Beaubien had only two blankets, which covered a man until he was asleep, then were removed for a newcomer. But Mark's Sauganash tavern became noted throughout the Northwest.

Save for the inns, there was not much town. The garrison of the fort departed, leaving Archibald Clybourn, its butcher, to open a store at Miller's tavern. James McKee stayed on as village blacksmith and mail rider, and the Rev. William See arrived to serve as Methodist parson. Billy Caldwell, Sauganash of the Potawatomis, had the only frame house in town, built for him by the government. Trade was sparse. Flour was milled in Plainfield, in Du Page County, or brought in by the steamship, *William Penn,* which also carried barreled pork, barreled whisky, and window sash. Now and then Hoosiers came up the Wabash Trace in their Conestoga wagons, fetching prod-

uce, driving pigs. They took back brown sheeting, salt, tar to grease their wagon wheels. Their corn brought only 10 cents a bushel, oats 5 cents, scarcely the cost of hauling it.

In 1832 an Indian war focused attention on Chicago and the Illinois country. It began when Black Hawk, the Sauk chieftain, denounced the encroachment of the whites upon the lands of his people and set out from Iowa to retake the ceded hunting grounds. Farmers flocked to the forts as he defeated the Illinois militia on May 14 and began savage raids on the settlements. Fort Dearborn, defended only by a militia, was packed with frightened people. Gurdon Hubbard volunteered to seek aid along the Wabash and rode one hundred and twenty miles to Danville in little more than a day. There he raised a company of 50 volunteers and started back. Meanwhile, General John R. Williams led a regiment of Michigan militia to Chicago, to hold the post until General Winfield Scott could arrive with his regulars.

Scott engaged four steamboats. But his soldiers were stricken with cholera and only the *Sheldon Thompson* reached Chicago from Detroit, arriving July 10. Sixteen of the passengers died en

In 1836, the taxpayers built Chicago's first public school at Madison and Dearborn streets. It was called the Rumsey school, for A. G. Rumsey, one of the teachers, employed at $33.33 a month. That same year Miss Francis L. Willard opened a private school for young ladies to succeed Miss Chappel's "infant school." *(Chicago Public Library.)*

Father John Mary Ireneaus St. Cyr erected St. Mary's, the town's first church building, on Lake Street west of State, at a cost of $400 in 1833. The Presbyterian and Baptist churches were built in 1834. *(Paulist Fathers.)*

route. Fort Dearborn became a hospital. The dead were cast into a great pit dug at Lake Street and Wabash Avenue. Overworked doctors could give the living scant attention. A sergeant carpenter, on burial detail, observed one victim stir as he was gathering corpses. "Sir," he remarked to the officer in charge, "this man is not ready to be buried yet." The stricken soldier revived in the open air and survived his woes.

By the end of July the cholera subsided and General Scott marched off in quest of Black Hawk. He was too late. The Illinois militia annihilated the Indians at Bad Axe River on August 2, and the war was over. General Scott urged the War Department to begin construction of a canal and harbor at Chicago.

Now the first Chicago boom began. Thousands of soldiers brought back excited reports of the fine lands in Illinois and Wisconsin. The Erie Canal, new roads, and railroads provided transportation West. In March 1833 Congress acted on the recommendation of a young army engineer, Jefferson Davis, and voted $25,000 to cut the sand bar and build a harbor at Chicago. Stagecoaches rolled in twice a week from Detroit, bringing land buyers.

A newcomer arriving in 1832 had been John

First public building in Chicago was an "estray pen" for straying animals. Later, on the same site in the town square, this log jail was built. It sometimes held 28 prisoners, but was not altogether satisfactory, as Sheriff Cook's reward notice indicates. Cook County's first courthouse was built at Clark and Randolph streets, near the jail, in 1835. The courtroom could seat 200 persons. *(Chicago Historical Society.)*

Stephen Wright, whose parents hoped to open a store in Galena. The Indian scare halted them at Chicago, and John, then seventeen, was put in charge of the oxen and store goods while his father continued west, seeking a likely site. John promptly began selling the goods from the oxcart. When a sale of government land was announced, he joined Philo Carpenter, newly arrived druggist and hardware merchant, in the purchase of two acres of swamp. Young Wright paid $25.00 for his share and made $1,000 on the rising prices by the time his father returned. Two years later, at nineteen, John Stephen Wright had $200,000 and a civic fervor that never died.

On August 5, 1833, the taxpayers voted to incorporate Chicago as a village. Five days later 18 of them turned out to elect the village trustees, 13 of the electors being candidates. The trustees shortly met to accept a square of land on Randolph Street from the state, where they erected a log prison. John Calhoun, a young printer, arrived to set up the first newspaper, the *Chicago Democrat*. The first issue, November 26, promised a strong partisan stand on all issues and reported the activities of the trustees. They had passed a code of ordinances which provided, among other things, that no hog was to run at large without a ring in the nose or a yoke about the neck. The fine for each offense would be $2.00.

There were 43 houses in Chicago and fewer than 200 inhabitants. But in 1831 the town had been made the seat of the new Cook County, extending to the Wisconsin line and named for Congressman Cook. The county began building roads and shortly the village borrowed $60.00 to drain and surface State Street. Colonel T. J. V. Owen, the new Indian agent succeeding Alexander Wolcott, organized a school in the R. J. Hamilton stable, north of the river, employing John Hawkins to teach in it in 1832. A year later, prospering John Wright built his Prairie store at Lake and Clark, named because of its remoteness from the village, and offered his old building on South Water Street as a school. Miss Elizabeth Chappel arrived to start classes, at Wright's expense. Young Wright helped the Rev. Jeremiah Porter organize the Presbyterian church, which met in the log school on the north side of the river. Later, in 1833, he helped Father John Mary Ireneaus St. Cyr erect St. Mary's Catholic Church, the first church building in the town. That same year P. W. F. Peck arrived to put up the first two-story frame building in town for his store on South Water Street where he sold salt, sugar, and hardware while he also bought and sold land.

The speculators now clamored for a clear title to the Indian lands. In 1833, Colonel Owen summoned the Potawatomis to Chicago to meet the

The State Street slough, probably south of State and Madison, where Henry Whitehead built the first State Street store in 1834. The undated picture may be a daguerreotype by John Plumbe, Jr., who learned the art in 1840 and later made pictures en route to Iowa. (*Chicago Historical Society.*)

government commissioners. Some 5,000 responded, camping about the town. "There were Potawatomis on all sides," reported Charles J. LaTrobe, an English traveler present. "They brought their squaws, children, ponies, and dogs and howled, sang, wept, and whooped in their various encampments. . . . The town was overrun with visitors, emigrants, land speculators as numerous as the sand, horse dealers and horse stealers, rogues of every description—white, black, brown, red—half-breeds, quarter-breeds, and men of no breed at all; dealers in pigs, poultry, potatoes, sharpers of every degree; pedlars, grog sellers, Indian agents and Indian traders of every description."

The Potawatomis, enjoying every minute of it at government expense, were in no hurry to get down to business. Finally, on September 21, they consented to meet the commissioners under a canopy in a meadow at South Water and Clark streets, where a spokesman inquired as to the purpose of the meeting.

Colonel Owen informed the assembled chiefs that they were being given an opportunity to sell their lands, since the Great Father had learned this was their wish. "Our Great Father listens to bad birds," replied the chiefs. They did not want to sell. The powwow was again delayed. But on September 25 the tribes capitulated. They met to sign the treaty, receiving, for 5,000,000 acres of land, $320,000 of annuities, $225,000 for schools, $125,000 in trade goods, and $285,-000 to pay off their debts—a provision that especially interested most of the whites. Within three years the Indians were to remove to an area west of the Mississippi, where the government would settle and support them for a year.

Much of this windfall was soon in the hands of the whites, inflating the boom. A parcel of land on Lake Street, sold for $300 early in 1833, shot

John D. Caton (top right) who saw last war dance of Potawatomis, and John Stephen Wright, Chicago booster. (*Authors' Collection.*)

Mastheads of Chicago's first newspapers: the *Democrat,* later absorbed by the *Tribune;* the *American,* with an inked-in June date line after it failed to appear May 8, as planned, and Wright's *Prairie Farmer.* (*Chicago Historical Society.*)

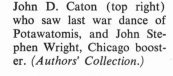

up to $60,000. Gurdon Hubbard bought a part interest in an acreage for $5,000, subdivided it, and sold his share for $100,000. By the winter of 1834 the population had doubled. Charles Fenno Hoffman, a New York editor, arrived to find everyone giddy with the land craze and talking of the new canal, to be started soon. A new stage line ran to St. Louis. The *Democrat* was attempting to interest the citizens in a railroad to connect with lines to the East. Farmers drove in cattle and pigs from the rich Des Plaines Valley. George W. Dole, Chicago agent of Oliver Newberry of Detroit, opened a slaughterhouse and made the first shipment of beef from Chicago, 287 barrels, plus 14 barrels of tallow and 152 hides. The cost of flour rose to $28.00 a barrel. The *Democrat* estimated the population at 9,000 by 1835 and reported 75 buildings erected.

In the midst of the boom the Indians gathered in Chicago for the last time. They came in the summer of 1835 to receive their annuities before departing West. "Some 5,000 assembled at the council house," reported John D. Caton, a lawyer in town. "Of these 800 were warriors. All were naked except for a strip of cloth around the loins. They were armed with tomahawks and war clubs, and were led by what answered for a band of music, which created a discordant din of hideous noises. They proceeded along the (north) bank of the river, not by a regular march, but by a dance, crossed the north branch, proceeded to the south branch bridge. Their eyes were wild and bloodshot. Their countenances expressed fierce anger, terrible hate and remorseless cruelty. With every step and gesture they uttered frightful yells, dancing with spasmodic steps, now forward with face and head thrown up, and now back or sideways. Their weapons they brandished as if they would slay a thousand enemies at every blow."

The dancing struck terror to the newcomers. "How easy it would have been for them to massacre us all!" Caton observed. But the Indians had come for their money. They danced down Lake Street, to the gates of Fort Dearborn, where they were paid, then departed to drink and howl throughout the night in their camp on Rush Street. After that, except for a few chiefs who had learned white men's ways, such as Billy Caldwell and Alexander Robinson, Chicago saw them no more. Even Ouilmette, the half-breed, departed to live on 800 acres granted to him north of town, where ultimately a suburb was named in his honor.

The old order had ended.

The last council of the Potawatomis, in which they ceded their northern Illinois lands in 1833. A mural by Lawrence C. Earle. *(Chicago Historical Society.)*

The Boomers and Boosters

V

The town was packed with people and the land fever raged. On June 8, 1835, when Thomas V. Davis began publication of the *Chicago American,* Chicago's second newspaper, he estimated that 2,000 transients were on hand, seeking land and jobs. More than 80 per cent of the resident population had arrived since the previous spring. The citizens were young, daring, optimistic, and they brought in money. William B. Ogden, turning thirty and a member of the New York legislature, arrived to look over land a relative had bought, and at first concluded that his kinsman had been swindled. Then he drained the acreage, sold half of it for $100,000, and hastily resigned from the legislature and his job as postmaster at Walton, New York, to stay in Chicago. Stephen A. Douglas, Vermont born, left his Jacksonville, Illinois, law practice to see Chicago, bought 1,000 acres of sand dunes south of town, and stayed to become a congressman and a senator. A young and eager lawyer, Joseph N. Balestier, reported that he averaged $500 a day for five successive days, just making out titles to land.

"The physicians threw physic to the dogs and wrote promissory notes instead of prescriptions," Balestier declared. "Even the day laborer became learned in the mysteries of quit-claim and warrantry. Few cared to work and the price of labor was exorbitant."

John Stephen Wright increased his fortune by $90,000 and found time to issue the first published map of Chicago. Gurdon S. Hubbard sold for $96,700 an acreage he had purchased for $67.00 in 1830. Walter L. Newberry ran a $1,000 North Side investment into half a million. Auctioneer John Augustus knocked down a total of $1,800,000 of town lots in a year.

As the land craze brought visitors, the innkeepers thrived. Mark Beaubien built a new hotel which he leased to John and Harriet Murphy as the United States-Sauganash. Thereafter he devoted himself to entertaining the guests and making money in real estate. Charles Taylor enlarged the Wolf Tavern and called it The Traveler's Home. James Kinzie built the Green Tree Tavern, Ashbel Steel opened the Eagle House, and John Davis launched the Steamboat Hotel. Meantime, Starr Foot was building the Tremont House at Lake and Dearborn, and on the north side of the river, at Rush Street, a syndicate led by Hubbard erected the three-story brick Lake House. Famed for its 50-foot bar and its unobstructed view of Lake Michigan, the Lake House soon attracted judges, politicians, land speculators, lake captains and gamblers, the elite of the town.

Speculation soared in June 1836 when $2,500,000 in canal lots were sold as construction of the canal was about to begin. William Ogden, who had taken a contract to build the Chicago segment of the ditch, imported Irish workers to do the digging. With the aid of the *American,* he led the town in the organization of a celebration to mark the start of work on July 4.

Early that morning hundreds of citizens gathered at the new Dearborn Street bridge to board the steamer *Chicago* and the schooners *Sea Serpent* and *Llewellyn* for free passage to Canalport. Others proceeded by wagon, buggy, and barouche

Chicago in 1845, from the southwest. Engraved for *J. W. Norris' Directory*, published in 1844.

Oliver Newberry, of Detroit, and George W. Dole, his Chicago agent, launched the young town into the export business via Newberry's fleet of lake vessels. In this sketch the *Osceola* is taking on Chicago's first shipment of grain in October 1839 at the Newberry and Dole dock on North Water Street. *Left:* George W. Dole. *(Chicago Historical Society.)*

A bridge quarrel split the town when North Siders demanded a span at Dearborn Street and South Siders opposed it, since they preferred to keep the Wabash Trace trade for themselves. The North Siders won, and in 1834 the first drawbridge was built, replacing the "grapevine" ferry. About 300 feet long, it opened 60 feet, but was frequently rammed by ships. In 1839, angry South Siders chopped it down just after the city council had voted to remove it. They feared North Siders would cause the council to revoke its action. *(Chicago Historical Society.)*

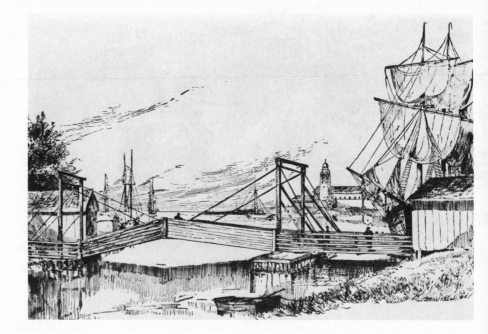

after 52 rounds of artillery had been fired in salute. At the site Simon Archer turned the first shovel of earth and Dr. William B. Egan and Gurdon S. Hubbard made speeches. Then several boxes of lemons were tossed into a nearby spring "to make lemonade for the temperance people." Finally, a barrel of whisky was added "to make punch for the rest of us." Late that afternoon, as the jolly throng started back, passengers on the *Chicago* were attacked by Bridgeport Irishmen, come to dig the ditch, who hurled rocks. The celebrants beached their boat, pursued and captured six of the rock throwers, and carried them back to jail.

The canal, to be 60 feet wide, 6 feet deep, and nearly 100 miles long, was finally under way. Calls went out for more workers, and immigrants arrived: 900 Irish, 800 Germans, Swedes, and Norwegians. The land boom roared on. When Harriet Martineau, the English writer, arrived in the winter of 1836, the city seemed to her to be the busiest on the continent. "The streets are crowded with land speculators," she wrote. "A Negro dressed in scarlet, bearing a scarlet flag, announced the time of the [land] sale. At every corner he stopped, the crowd flocked around him

and it seemed as if some of the prevalent mania infected the whole people. . . . As the gentlemen of our party walked the streets, storekeepers hailed them from doors with offers of farms and all manner of corner lots."

New stores and houses went up along La Salle, Clark, and Dearborn streets, spreading the town south and west. John Kinzie, son of the pioneer; James Kinzie II, his nephew, and Gurdon Hubbard erected fine brick homes on South Michigan Avenue, facing the lake. Ogden, a bachelor, built a mansion on Ontario Street, where he entertained notables. At La Salle and Water streets Gurdon Hubbard raised a huge brick packing house, called "Hubbard's Folly" because of its size, where he packed and stored 5,000 hogs for the opening of spring navigation. Captain J. B. F. Russell's three-story brick Saloon Building at Lake and Clark streets was the town's pride. Here Chicago was incorporated as a city on March 4, 1837. And here William Ogden, elected mayor on the Democratic ticket in a campaign against John Kinzie, presided over the city council meetings as panic deflated the boom.

The panic of 1837 came suddenly, and hit hard. Banks crashed throughout the Northwest, leaving

Construction of the Illinois and Michigan Canal began July 4, 1836. These canal barges were converted to excursion boats for the canal opening ceremonies in 1847. *(Chicago Public Library.)*

a wreckage littered with their wildcat notes. Chicago businessmen bartered, and issued their own scrip. The state of Illinois went bankrupt, and the new city of Chicago seemed certain to follow. But Mayor Ogden would not permit it. "Bankruptcy is a disgrace!" he yelled at a council meeting, then borrowed money on his personal credit and used it to pay city bills. Work on the canal stopped, speculators failed. John Stephen Wright, one of the victims, lost his fortune and set out to make another in the shipping and commission business. Others, such as Ogden and Peck, and Walter Newberry were able to hold their lands and to buy more. Calhoun, owner of the *Democrat,* sold a half-interest to Long John Wentworth. Davis, equally in trouble, sold his *American* to William Stuart.

Speculation stalled as prices hit bottom, but now the real wealth of the Northwest began to reach Chicago. Cattle, hogs, and provisions moved up the Wabash Trace and eastward from the Rock River and southward from Wisconsin to the slaughterhouses on the Chicago River. By night Wabash Avenue at the river was a great, roaring camp where drovers and Conestoga wagoners gathered around their fires. When the river was frozen, Hubbard, Archibald Clybourn, and other packers piled the carcasses of hogs and beef on the ice until they were frozen solid, then stored them in their warehouses. Farmers from the Des Plaines, Fox, and Illinois River valleys hauled in their

grain. On October 8, 1839, as the panic was ending, Newberry and Dole shipped 1,678 bushels of wheat by the brig *Osceola,* the beginning of grain export for the town that was to become the world's great provisioner.

Men wiped out by panic were ready to try again. "I came to Chicago with nothing, failed for $100,000. . . . I could have failed for a million!" exclaimed John Stephen Wright. He was buying land again, and planning a newspaper designed to help the farmers, "the true source of Chicago's potential wealth." He would call it the *Prairie Farmer.* John Wentworth's *Democrat* was filled with optimism and slogans as the new editor demanded government money for Chicago improvements and convinced the voters that they should send him to Congress to get it. William Ogden quietly invited English and Dutch financiers into town, showed them the possibilities, and brought in foreign capital.

Planners and boosters were needed. The town's reputation was bad. Thousands outside the city had been hurt in the collapse of the land bubble. Rival cities called Chicago a mudhole, a pigsty, a sinkhole of vice and gambling. John Hankins, leader of the Washingtonians, a Temperance movement, roared in to declare Chicago the vilest city he had seen, "a universal grogshop." Liquor consumption was high. Even the American Temperance House had a bartender, one George Cook, according to the city directory. Saloons and brothels stretched along Wells Street. The Sands, on the north side of the river, was a warren of gambling hells, vice dens, and barrel houses. Only New Orleans and the big eastern cities had more gambling places.

It was true that Chicago was a mudhole and many of the lots sold to outsiders were under water most of the year. There were weeks when mud closed all the roads and wagoners could neither get in nor out. On the worst days as many as 160 prairie schooners would be marooned at State and South Water streets. Carriages and drays were frequently abandoned in the muddy ways. Women rode in carts with high sideboards to avoid splashing. Shacks and sidewalks were built on stilts, and often crashed when their supports sank into the mire.

But the rude pioneer town had spirit. When in 1839 the government's Fort Dearborn land was ordered sold, and it became known that stubborn old Jean Beaubien might lose his homestead, the citizens banded together and agreed not to bid. The pact was upset by an outlander, James H. Collins, whose offer was accepted. Townsmen held an indignation meeting, resolving: "That the man who would thus render homeless and houseless this old man . . . deserves now the execration of all honest men." But the sale stood and Beaubien departed to spend the rest of his days with his Potawatomi friends.

Despite the difficult times, there was sport and recreation. Hunting was good in the surrounding marshes. Guests occasionally shot wild ducks from the porch of the Tremont House and noon-hour hunting forays along State Street were common. In winter wolves howled within a mile of the town. The young men organized expeditions to the stage-line taverns beyond the city or canoe trips to see "Juliet" mountain near Joliet, to the south. Women were in great demand, said the *Democrat,* which promised an attractive marriage for any girl who came to town. Charles Fenno Hoffman, attending a cotillion, marveled at its color and dash. "The band consisted of a dandy Negro with his violin, a fine military-looking bass drummer from the fort, and a volunteer citizen, who alternately played an accompaniment upon the flute and triangle. . . . Here you might see a veteran officer in full uniform balancing to a tradesman's daughter still in her short frock and trousers, while there the golden aiguilettes of a handsome surgeon [Dr. Philip Maxwell] flapped in unison with the glass beads upon a scrawny neck of fifty. In one quarter the high-placed buttons of a linsey-woolsey coat would be *dos á dos* to the elegantly turned shoulders of a delicate-looking southern girl; and in another, a pair of Cinderella-like slippers would *chassez* cross with a brace of thick-soled broghans."

By 1843 Chicago had a population of 7,590 and 691 vessels cleared the port. Wheat exports totaled 628,967 bushels, flour 10,786 barrels. Ogden was attempting to interest the businessmen in a railroad, and to resume work on the canal. Wentworth, in Congress, was battling for funds

John Frink and Martin O. Walker operated their stagecoaches from the corner of Lake and Dearborn streets. Lathrop Johnson ran the first stage, to Milwaukee, in 1834. The trip took twenty-four hours. By 1845, eight stages arrived and departed each day, to Peoria, Galena, Detroit, and Milwaukee. Fare to Milwaukee, $3.00 in summer and $5.00 in winter, when an overnight stop was required. *(Chicago Historical Society.)*

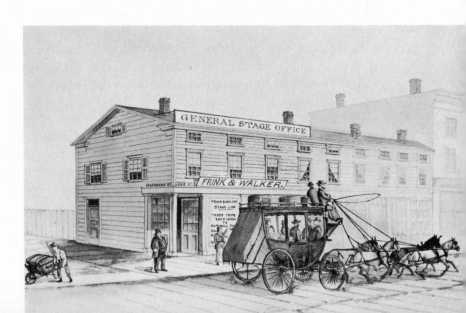

Starr Foot built the first Tremont House at the northwest corner of Lake and Dearborn streets in 1834. Next door, James and Ira Couch kept a tailor shop in a 6-by-9-foot room. Two years later the Couch brothers took over the hotel. After it was razed by fire in 1839, they built another Tremont House, shown above, on the southeast corner. The third Tremont House was built of brick in 1850, and a fourth arose after the fire of 1871. *(Chicago Sun-Times Library.)*

to improve the harbor and staving off Wisconsin's attempts to reclaim northern Illinois and its promising port town. The offer of a senatorship by Wisconsin politicians failed to seduce Wentworth. The move failed. Wentworth's harbor bill passed, then was vetoed by President James Polk.

There was an uproar in the Northwest, especially at Chicago, where Ogden had the canal work under way again and better harbor facilities would soon be needed. At the suggestion of William Hall, agent of the Lake Steamboat Association, Wentworth called for a meeting of delegates to a Rivers and Harbors Convention in Chicago the summer of 1847. The issue was clear, he said. It was now to be the Northwest against the South in a ferocious fight for western trade. Chicago spruced up and prepared for its visitors.

The response to the convention call astounded even Wentworth. In July more than 3,000 delegates from 18 of the 29 states traveled to Chicago at their own expense. On Sunday, July 4, there was a great parade as the town assembled every available wagon and cart to present floats depicting the history and growth of the city and the

Northwest. More than 16,000 watched as bands, military companies, marching clubs, firemen, and delegates themselves proceeded down Randolph Street. Eastern dignitaries present especially excited the crowd. There was Horace Greeley, editor of the *New York Tribune;* Erastus Corning, president of the New York Central Railroad; Thurlow Weed, Albany editor and boss of the New York Whigs; Senator Tom Corwin of Ohio, prime foe of President Polk.

The convention, non-partisan but definitely anti-South, came to order on Monday in a big tent pitched in Dearborn Park on Randolph Street. Thurlow Weed declared it was the largest deliberative body ever assembled. For three days the delegates discussed their problems and passed resolutions. They wanted federal funds for internal improvements and federal support for railroads, especially a great railway west, to run north of the area of southern influence. Chicago would be its natural eastern terminus.

President Polk and Congress ignored the Chicago convention, but the East did not. Editors and writers sent back glowing reports on the

Captain J. B. F. Russell erected the three-story brick Saloon Building at the southeast corner of Lake and Clark streets in 1836. On the third floor was the largest assembly hall west of Buffalo. The city of Chicago was organized here March 4, 1837, and for five years the Saloon Building served as a city hall. Stephen Douglas had his first debate there in 1838. *(Chicago Historical Society.)*

West Lake Street, called "Rotten Row," as it appeared in 1843. Chicagoans at the time bought their drinking water from vendors who delivered it in barrels. W. E. S. Trowbridge drawing. *(Chicago Historical Society.)*

city's prospects. "In ten years Chicago will be as big as Albany," Thurlow Weed told the readers of his *Albany Journal.* "On the shores of this lake is a vast country that will in fifty years support a city of 125,000 inhabitants."

The convention was a tremendous success for Chicago. New business ventures were launched as eastern capital flowed in. A system of plank roads was started and promptly began paying investors 32 per cent on their money. Ogden, pushing his plans for a railroad to Galena, got added

capital and there was talk of other lines to the southwest and east. Cyrus Hall McCormick, thirty-eight-year-old inventor of a reaping machine, came to look over the town. He borrowed $100,000 from Ogden and in partnership with Charles M. Gray built a big, steam-powered factory on the north side of the river where the Kinzie house stood. Within a year his factory was employing 120 men who turned out hundreds of reapers.

Said William Bross, the new Chicago booster:

81

Worst of the frequent floods that inundated Chicago occurred March 12, 1849, when the Des Plaines River spilled across Mud Lake, beaching and wrecking more than 100 ships. This drawing is after a daguerreotype by F. von Schneidnau. (*Chicago Historical Society.*)

"The Rivers and Harbors Convention has given Chicago her second greatest impulse, the first being the start of the canal in 1836."

And finally the Illinois and Michigan canal was ready. It opened with a celebration and ceremonies on April 16, 1848. On the first day, 16 vessels passed through. Now farmers could haul their grain to port towns along the route. Sugar came up all the way from New Orleans, cotton from Memphis. Lines of canal barges packed the Chicago River, taking on clothing and manufactured goods from the East, lumber from the North for their return trip. Warehouses and lumberyards spread along the branches of the river. Slips were dug to accommodate more boats.

A few months later Ogden's railroad was complete to the Des Plaines River, ten miles away. On November 20, 1848, the first train went out, the secondhand locomotive, Pioneer, pulling secondhand cars over secondhand strap rails. The next week 30 wagonloads of wheat awaited shipment at the Des Plaines.

Within three years the Galena and Chicago Union eclipsed the new canal as a wheat carrier and promoters launched a new rail line, the Chicago and Rock Island, which would parallel the canal to Peru, then turn west to Rock Island on the Mississippi. Senator Douglas and bewhiskered Sidney A. Breese pressed their vast project,

the Illinois Central Railroad, called by many "the St. Louis cutoff." Ground for the new road was broken in Chicago and Cairo, in southern Illinois, on December 23, 1851. By 1856 the line was finished and Illinois Central trains ran downtown on trestles to the new station and yards between Randolph and Lake streets.

Meanwhile, two eastern lines pushed toward Chicago, the Michigan Central around the lake from Buffalo, and the Michigan Southern, coming up from Elkhart, Indiana, the latter arriving in Chicago February 20, 1852. The Pittsburgh, Fort Wayne, and Chicago, third great line to the East, ran its first train from Pittsburgh to Chicago on Christmas Day, 1858. By that year Stephen H. Gale's Aurora Branch Railroad had been extended all the way to Quincy and Ogden had put together a group of roads to tap the rich Wisconsin farm country as well as western Illinois.

Prospects were never better. By 1853, the population was 60,652. Chicago shipped 6,000,000 bushels of grain, boasted 27 miles of planked streets, 59 miles of sidewalks, four miles of wharves, 56 miles of sewers, ten bridges, a gasworks, and street lamps. In 1854 a new waterworks was built, additions were laid out until the city covered 18 square miles. As the new railroads came in, and the Soo Canal opened in 1855, business jumped. Chicago became the world's

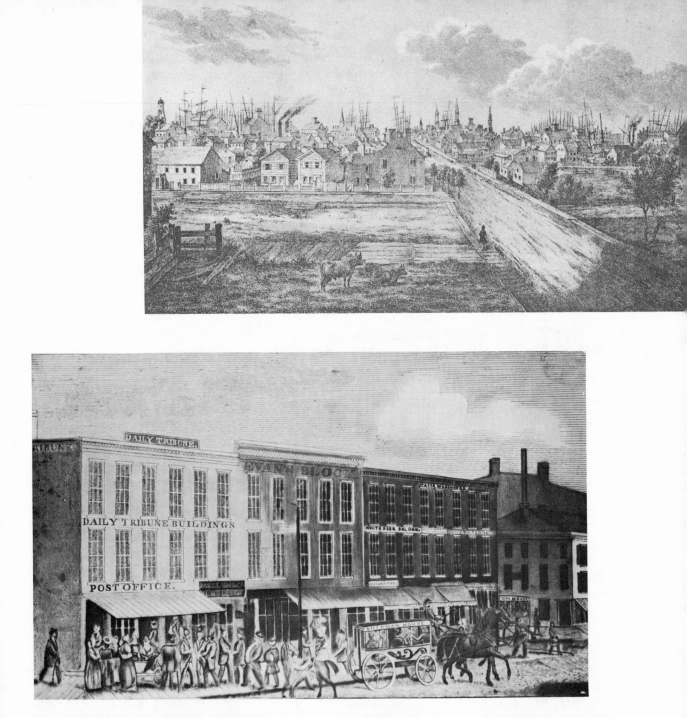

Top. Chicago's near North Side in 1849, looking south along State Street from the College of St. Mary's of the Lake. *(New York Public Library.)*

Joseph Medill, of Cleveland (left), joined Charles Ray, newly arrived from Galena, in the purchase of the *Chicago Daily Tribune,* and proceeded to expand its circulation and influence from rooms over the post office, on Clark Street's Newspaper Row (above). *(Chicago Tribune Library.)*

John Blake Rice, a Maryland actor, built his first theater on Dearborn Street, near Randolph, in June 1847, opened an $11,000 brick theater in 1851. Leading stage stars visited Chicago, but much entertainment was of a home-talent variety, presented in the Saloon Building hall, or at Rice's, or Tremont Hall. *(Chicago Historical Society.)*

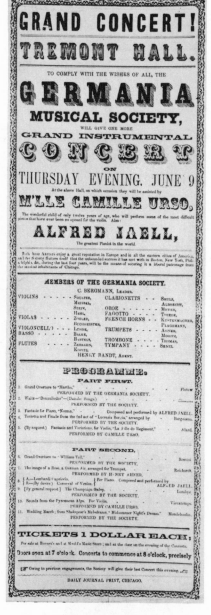

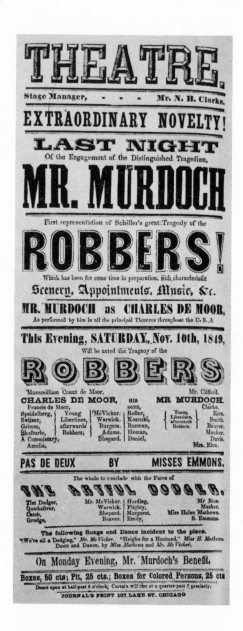

biggest lumber market. It shipped 12,000,000 bushels of wheat in 1854 and 21,000,000 bushels in 1856. "Chicago is the greatest primary market in the world," exulted William Bross. "We exceed St. Louis by 250 per cent, Milwaukee by 400 per cent."

By 1855 there were 2,933 miles of railroad tracks touching Chicago, ten trunk lines, and 11 branch lines. Ninety-six trains a day entered or left the city. On a single day the Michigan Central hauled 3,400 immigrants into town. When the Toronto Board of Trade members arrived to see for themselves, they found a city of 84,000 people, seven daily newspapers, 15 weeklies, two telegraph lines, 57 hotels. They were told that in a year Chicago cleared 107,653 emigrants for the West, men and women who soon would be shipping grain and hogs to Chicago and buying its manufactures.

The changes were vast and sometimes troublesome. Crime increased, impoverished immigrants overtaxed the aid societies. The immigrants, though necessary, were resented and often exploited and misunderstood. A minor war ensued in 1855 when Mayor Levi Boone, ignoring the established habits of the Germans, ordered the saloons, including the German beer gardens, closed on Sundays. When 200 saloonkeepers were arrested, mobs of Germans invaded the downtown area. In a gunfight, a rioter was killed, a policeman and several others wounded, and some 80 rioters arrested.

In 1857, with Long John Wentworth in the mayor's chair, crime became so rampant that he decided personally to exterminate its stronghold, The Sands, in a mass raid. On April 20, Wentworth organized a raiding party of 30 policemen. They crossed the river in boats and drove out the gamblers, madams, and inmates of the crib houses and saloons. The police destroyed nine buildings, and fire which broke out later razed six more. While some complained that the prostitutes had been driven into respectable parts of the town, or asserted that the mayor acted for William Ogden, new owner of The Sands, Long John's forthright methods were widely hailed about the country. A few weeks later Mayor Wentworth led another

Mystics, quacks, and patent-medicine fakirs were popular in the new town. The Chicago Phrenological Society had a large and avid following, mostly of women. Dogfights, cockfights, and bare-fist battles, with both men and women as adversaries, amused the rougher element. Men suffered no intrusion in their barbershops, sacred to talk of politics, sports, and corner lots. Beauty shops for women were not yet known. Barber prices were modest, as indicated below. *(Chicago Historical Society.)*

The Pioneer, which ran ten miles to the Des Plaines River on strap-iron rails, initiated Chicago's reign as the world's greatest railroad center in 1848. Above, the Galena and Chicago Union's original Pioneer locomotive, with reconstructed tender and coach. *(Chicago and North Western.)*

First Chicago railroad station, built on the west side of the Chicago River's north branch at Kinzie Street (opposite the present Merchandise Mart) by the Galena and Chicago Union in 1848. It later became a reading room for railroad employees. *(Chicago and North Western.)*

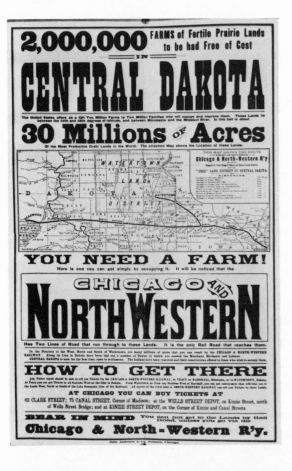

The Galena and Chicago Union never reached Galena, but became the Chicago and North Western as William Ogden extended his line westward and acquired feeder lines that tapped the granaries of the Northwest. By 1854, the North Western served an area indicated by the map shown at left, which was printed on the back of the system's hat checks. The front of the hat check, slipped into a passenger's hatband to indicate his fare had been checked by the conductor, is shown at top left. The poster is one of thousands distributed by the railroad to attract settlers to its territories, bringing thousands to cheap lands and government homesteads. Farmers soon shipped grain and pigs to Chicago, got back manufactured goods from the city's growing wholesale houses. Below is a detail of the strap-iron rails used on the first line to the Des Plaines River. *(Chicago and North Western.)*

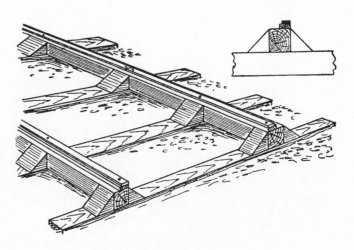

raid, this time against the gamblers and sharpers along Randolph Street. He personally saw his victims jailed, then locked up a lawyer who arrived to talk to them. For a time the town's crooks took cover. Then Wentworth staged his third raid, against merchants and vendors who ignored his order to keep their signs and crates off the sidewalks. This time he was denounced as a tyrant, and his days in the city hall were numbered.

While Wentworth was stirring up the town, new disaster struck. Panic, rolling in from the East, caught merchants with heavy inventories, industrialists short of orders, closed the private banking house of E. R. Hinckly and Company on July 3. Soon there was a heavy run on Hoffman's bank, the bank of R. K. Swift, Brother and Company, and the Cherokee Banking and Insurance Company. All three closed their doors. Work was suspended on half-finished buildings, prices fell, men were jobless, a total of 117 Chicago business firms were in ruin. On October 19, fire starting in a brothel swept the stores on South Water and Lake streets. At a mass funeral for the 21 victims, the Rev. W. W. King, of St. Paul's Church, intoned: "What we have just witnessed is but a slight breaking out of the volcanic fires burning under our feet. It is shameful to witness that complicity between authority and vice and crime by which our city is cursed and degraded."

But again Chicago was equal to calamity. Along Lake Street merchants reduced their inventories in distress sales and fire sales and soon called on the wholesalers and factories for new goods. Potter Palmer, the young Quaker merchant, announced that he would move into a new five-story marble front, and would also launch a wholesale business. Other businessmen followed him. They knew at last that the canal and railroads had changed Chicago from a farmer's retail market to a wholesale and manufacturing center. They sent out traveling salesmen to capture the wholesale trade from St. Louis, Cincinnati, and Toledo; Galena no longer counted. And the new and greatest boom was about to begin.

A rare photograph of Chicago's first horse railroad, which began operating in State Street in 1858. The scene is State and Randolph streets, with the Tobey Furniture Company on the northeast corner. The horse-car line reached Cottage Grove Avenue in time to carry passengers to the fair of 1859. (*Chicago Historical Society.*)

VI

"Queen of the North and the West"

By 1860, Chicago was beginning to win the long struggle for dominance of the Northwest. The town's 15 railroads tapped the trade of Kansas and Missouri and monopolized Iowa, Nebraska, the Dakotas, and everything north. Its three dozen wholesale houses dispatched their drummers to invade the territories of St. Louis and Cincinnati. Their orders kept nearly 500 Chicago factories busy and exports rose to new peaks. Cincinnati still led in pork packing. St. Louis forwarded more livestock and leather. New Orleans garnered a greater share of the mid-continent trade. But Chicago ran them all a close second. It sneered at St. Louis as "a fur-trade town," at Cincinnati as "old and decrepit," and insisted effete New Orleans would perish were it not for the lively center on the Great Lakes end of the Lakes-Gulf trade axis. In defense of "The Queen of the Lakes" Deacon Bross and John Stephen Wright kept up a barrage of statistical fire, to which the newspapers contributed a bombardment of vituperation.

The political struggle was no less harsh. Nathaniel Pope had been right when he predicted that a harbor and canal at Chicago would help to give the North control of the West. Northern emigrants settled in Illinois. Chicago railroads carried thousands all the way to Kansas and Missouri. Trade was diverted to the Great Lakes. Illinois, once southern, was split. Here the final battle for men's minds was fought. Both parties turned to the battleground for leaders in the time of crisis: Abraham Lincoln, the Springfield lawyer, tall, spare, and melancholic; Stephen A. Douglas, the

squat, intense senator from Chicago, idol of the Democrats.

In April, Democratic Chicago razed Mark Beaubien's old Sauganash Tavern on Lake Street to make a place for the Republican Wigwam, a pineboard political hall designed to accommodate 10,000 delegates and visitors to the Republican national convention. The *Tribune* had led Illinois newspapers in support of Lincoln for the nomination. Chicago had little doubt of the outcome.

Senator Douglas seemed even more certain of first place on the Democratic ticket. A compromiser but a fighter, he appeared to be the only man capable of holding his party together. At the Democratic convention in Charleston, South Carolina, in April, this prospect was dashed. Dixie delegates walked out. The convention was adjourned to a later meeting in Baltimore.

Early in May, Illinois Republicans meeting at Decatur agreed to back Lincoln. His chief strategists, led by David Davis of Bloomington, then hurried to Chicago, where they set up headquarters in the Tremont House and prepared to deal with the opposition. New York, led by Thurlow Weed, arrived in full strength to back its favorite son, Senator William H. Seward. Trainloads of easterners appeared with their marching clubs and bands. The Illinois men waited. The first two days of the convention were devoted to routine business. On the third, Friday, May 18, with nominations scheduled, the Lincoln strategists issued thousands of bogus tickets to their followers. While Sewardites paraded, the Lincoln men packed the hall.

89

Above. Chicago's lake front in the sixties, when sailboats skimmed the Michigan Avenue lagoon and troops drilled on the greensward that is now Grant Park. At right, the Illinois Central tracks. (*Jevne and Almini Print*.)

Left. On the morning of November 8, 1860, the steamer *Globe* exploded at Hale's dock, Clark and Wells streets, killing the crew of 25 and blasting debris through the roofs of buildings eight blocks away. (*Chicago Historical Society*.)

Below. Near midnight, September 8, 1860, the steamship *Lady Elgin* was returning from Chicago to Milwaukee with a party of excursionists. The lumber schooner *Augusta*, running without lights, struck her amidships and the *Lady Elgin* sank off Waukegan with a loss of 297 of the 393 men, women, and children aboard. (*The New York Illustrated News*.)

There were brawls as the Seward crowd fought to enter. Only official Seward delegates were seated; there was no room for Thurlow Weed's cheering sections. Speeches began and Seward was first to be nominated. Shouts from his delegates were drowned by the "Lincoln yawp" that reverberated from every part of the hall. Norman Judd of Chicago nominated Lincoln, and the din increased. William L. Dayton of New Jersey and Salmon P. Chase of Ohio were named. At this point, Caleb Smith of Indiana interrupted to second Lincoln. Sewardites stopped their ears as Lincoln men whooped it up. When the uproar ceased, Ohio seconded Lincoln, and the noise resumed. Finally, Simon Cameron of Pennsylvania and Supreme Court Justice John McLean of Chicago were nominated. This last move failed to divide the Lincoln men. They howled again: "Honest Abe, the Rail Splitter!"

The balloting began. The first roll call gave Seward 173½, Lincoln, 102; the rest were scattered. In the second roll call, Lincoln gained, Seward gained, then Lincoln drew ahead. When the vote stood at 231½ for Lincoln, with 233 needed to nominate, Joseph Medill, sitting with the Ohio delegation, whispered to David Cartter, Ohio chairman: "If you can throw Ohio to Lincoln, you can have anything you want!"

Cartter rose to change four Ohio votes to Lincoln. There was a silence. Then came that "Lincoln yawp" again. Delegates yelled and cheered and stomped. A cannon was fired on the Wigwam's roof. Boat whistles replied. Church bells rang. Newspaper telegraphers began pounding their keys. Lincoln was the man.

A few days later the Democratic convention reconvened in the Front Street Theater in Baltimore. The southern bolters were denied admission and the convention, after adopting the Douglas platform, proceeded to nominate the man who had long experience in battling Lincoln. Senator Douglas received 190 votes, all but 17 of those cast. The bolters held their own convention and named John C. Breckinridge of Kentucky for

Chicago, though Democratic, was a center of abolitionism in 1860. To welcome the Republican national convention, certain to nominate pro-northern candidates, the town built the Republican Wigwam at Lake and Market streets. It had seats for 5,000, but was packed by twice that number on the third day of the convention. A photograph by Alexander Hesler. (*Chicago Historical Society.*)

president. The Democrats were fatally split. Douglas stumped the country, unprecedented for a presidential candidate. Lincoln remained at home and won by a million fewer votes than were cast for his combined opponents.

A few weeks later, South Carolina voted to secede and sent commissioners to Washington to treat with President Buchanan. Douglas began a desperate campaign to keep his southern friends from following the radicals. As inauguration day approached, the "Little Giant" pledged his loyalty to Lincoln and the Union and denounced secession as criminal. But the movement spread. There was panic in the North as the South cut banking ties and canceled mill orders.

Then, on April 12, at 4:30 A.M., the bombardment of Fort Sumter began. Among the cities responding to President Lincoln's call for volunteers, Chicago furnished 3,500 men the first three weeks. But the financial panic increased. Some 6,000 businesses went down—more than were lost in the debacle of 1857. Of all its 110 banks, only 17 were open in Illinois. Chicago land prices plummeted as business stood still. Douglas sped through the border states and into southern Illinois, pleading for loyalty to the Union. He was heavily involved in Chicago properties and was unable to meet his mortgages, but he put the Union ahead of his personal problems. Weary, ill, and overburdened, he returned to Chicago that May. A month later, June 3, he was dead. President Lincoln ordered national mourning for the man "who nobly discarded party for his country." More than 70,000 Illinois citizens passed the body of the "Little Giant" as it lay in state; 10,000 marched in his funeral procession.

The months drew on. The North geared its economy to war. Strategically placed on water and rail transportation, Chicago was besieged with

Delegates arriving for Republican 1860 convention, sketched by W. B. Baird. *(Harper's Weekly.)*

Republicans assembled in the Wigwam convention that nominated Abraham Lincoln as a candidate for the presidency in May 1860. (*Harper's Weekly.*)

war orders which eastern investors were eager to finance. Soon the city was supplying the troops of Illinois, Iowa, Wisconsin, and Minnesota and the Army of the Cumberland was drawing upon the quartermaster depot in Chicago. Prices shot up. A new national banking act stabilized currency. In three months of 1862 Chicago killed and dressed 300,000 hogs. By the end of the year it had tripled Cincinnati's pork production, and grain shipments had jumped from 16,000,000 bushels to 65,000,000 bushels. More than 3,000 men were employed in the new boot and shoe industry, once virtually a St. Louis monopoly.

As men were drawn from the farms to the armies, the sale of McCormick reapers soared. Secretary of War Stanton credited them with being worth an army in the field. Thirty meat packers worked their plants day and night to keep the North supplied with pork and beef. Brewers increased their output 300 per cent. New fortunes were being made. The town expanded by 20 square miles as more factories and warehouses

93

Chicago's first war hero was the dashing Colonel Elmer E. Ellsworth, whose fast-stepping Chicago Zouaves won the drill championship of the United States and Canada in 1860. Prior to the outbreak of war, Ellsworth quit as drillmaster at Lake Forest Academy to train Illinois militia troops, then returned to his native New York where he formed the New York Zouaves. On May 24, 1861, Colonel Ellsworth led his company to Alexandria, Virginia. Seeing a Confederate flag flying on the Marshall Hotel, Colonel Ellsworth personally hauled it down. He was shot dead by James W. Jackson, the hotel manager, who was in turn slain by Ellsworth's troops. Colonel Ellsworth (left) was the first Union officer killed in the war. President Lincoln wept when he heard the news. Ellsworth's Chicago cadets, shown above receiving their colors and below with field arms, were in great demand as drill officers, and many of them distinguished themselves in the war. *(Chicago Public Library.)*

MULLIGAN'S BRIGADE!

LAST CHANCE TO AVOID THE DRAFT!

$402 BOUNTY!
TO VETERANS!

$302 to all other VOLUNTEERS!

All Able-bodied Men, between the ages of 18 and 45 Years, who have heretofore served not less than nine months, who shall re-enlist for Regiments in the field, will be deemed Veterans, and will receive one month's pay in advance, and a bounty and premium of $402. To all other recruits, one month's pay in advance, and a bounty and premium of $302 will be paid.

All who wish to join Mulligan's Irish Brigade, now in the field, and to receive the munificent bounties offered by the Government, can have the opportunity by calling at the headquarters of

CAPT. J. J. FITZGERALD

Of the Irish Brigade, 23d Regiment Illinois Volunteers, Recruiting Officer, Chicago, Illinois

Each Recruit, Veteran or otherwise, will receive

Seventy-five Dollars Before Leaving General Rendezvous,

and the remainder of the bounty in regular instalments till all is paid. The pay, bounty and premium for three years will average $24 per month, for Veterans; and $21.30 per month for all others.

If the Government shall not require these troops for the full period of Three Years, and they shall be mustered honorably out of the service before the expiration of their term of enlistment, they shall receive UPON BEING MUSTERED OUT, the whole amount of BOUNTY remaining unpaid, the same as if the full term had been served.

J. J. FITZGERALD,

Chicago, December, 1863.   Recruiting Officer, corner North Clark & Kinzie Streets

Senator Douglas and Long John Wentworth had made Democrats of Chicago's Irish as soon as they were eligible to vote, and it was feared they might not support the northern cause. But when war came, and Douglas and Wentworth vigorously backed the north, the Irish did, too, rallying to Colonel James A. Mulligan, another local hero. Mulligan and his entire first regiment were captured in Missouri, but he escaped and formed a new brigade in 1863. He and his troops fought valiantly in the Shenandoah Valley, where he was killed. The doughty colonel is shown above with his staff and below with a part of his brigade. *(Chicago Public Library.)*

Troops were raised by the bounty method, veterans receiving extra money when they re-enlisted. Not until the late months of the war was a draft needed in Chicago. *(Chicago Historical Society.)*

sprang up. Iron and brass foundries were built and Chicago became the meeting place of Lake Superior ore and southern Illinois coal.

Despite the profit-taking, Chicago contributed heavily to the northern cause. Of its 110,000 population at the beginning of the war, 15,000 men were in the armed services. Any fears that the foreign-born would not support the war proved groundless: immigrant Irish and German and Swede regiments were ahead of the native Americans in their enthusiasm for enlistment. A system of bonus payments, widely used and abused, delayed a draft call in Chicago until the third year of the war. The town contributed more than $4,000,000 to war activities, in addition to its federal taxes. Much of the money was raised through sanitary fairs, said to be the biggest and most successful in the country.

Although President Lincoln himself ranked Chicago as one of the foremost cities in support of the war, the city was infested with southern sympathizers. Not only were many of the leading families southern born, but after the outbreak of hostilities, river gamblers, criminals, and deserters flocked to town to escape Confederate military service and to share in the wartime prosperity. They were loud in praise of the land they had abandoned and they had a bold and fiery spokes-

SOLDIERS' FAIR!
Grand Musical Raffle!
500 TICKETS, $5.00 EACH.

FIRST PRIZE.—Chickering Marquetrie Piano, elaborately carved, inlaid with various kinds of woods, finished with Bronze Medallions, etc., constituting the finest Piano ever brought into the State.
Donated by Reed's Temple of Music, valued at................................$ 2,000.00

SECOND PRIZE—Shoninger Organ, five octave, double reed, six stops and Fancy Walnut Case.
Donated by Root & Cady, valued at ....$ 250.00

THIRD PRIZE.—Piano Cased Rosewood Melodeon, manufactured and donated by W. W. Kimball.
Valued at $250.00

FOURTH PRIZE.—Rosewood Guitar, patent head, etc., donated by Molter & Wurlitzer.
Valued at ....$ 25.00

☞ The above Instruments are GIVEN to the Fair, and all money received by the sale of the tickets goes for the benefit of the Soldiers.

☞ All Tickets unsold will be destroyed and not counted in the drawing, which will take place whether all the Tickets are sold or not.

☞ Time, place and manner of drawing has not yet been decided upon by the committee.

☞ REMEMBER—Winter is coming, and FIVE HUNDRED Soldiers, Soldiers' Widows and Orphans are in our city, in need of Wood and Coal, in need of Clothing, in need of Food. They must freeze and starve unless they have aid. No man is the poorer for what he gives to a cause like this.

Rounds & James, Printers, 46 State Street.

Chicago staged mammoth bazaars and benefits to raise funds for ambulances, canteens, and comforts in the field. The Northwestern Sanitary Fair was the country's most successful, raising $85,000. A second fair brought total receipts from such benefits to $358,000. War relics were shown, entertainment provided, personal possessions of war heroes auctioned off. One of the most successful fund-raising devices was the lottery. (*Chicago Historical Society*.)

Above. The Sanitary Fairs provided ambulances and medical supplies for the troops. Also widows, wives, and children received a portion of the funds. *(Illinois Historical Society.) Below.* Although the city was preoccupied with the war, it found time to assemble the National Ship Canal Convention to press for better water transportation. In 1865, the city began deepening the Illinois and Michigan canal to eight and one-half feet. When the work was finished at a cost of $3,000,-000, the current of the Chicago River was reversed from east to west. *(Chicago Historical Society.)*

Allan Pinkerton, the town's only police detective in 1850, won the confidence of President Lincoln early in the war when he discovered a plot to assassinate the President in Baltimore. In April 1861, President Lincoln invited Pinkerton to confer on the subject of a secret-service department. Pinkerton served in plain clothes throughout the war. His secret service proved its worth when operatives uncovered a Confederate plot to free the 8,000 Confederate prisoners in Camp Douglas, (shown below) on Chicago's South Side.

To forward this fantastic scheme, Captain Thomas H. Hines and four other Confederate officers entered the city in 1864, met local Copperheads at the Richmond Hotel, stored a supply of arms at the home of Charles Walsh. John T. Shanks was to lead an assault on the main gate, Colonel G. St. Leger Grenfel would issue arms to the prisoners and seize the courthouse square. The plot collapsed when it developed that Shanks was a Union secret-service agent. The conspirators were sentenced to prison. A group of Confederate prisoners at Camp Douglas is shown at the right. *(Chicago Historical Society.)*

Left. Pinkerton with Lincoln and General John A. McClernand at Antietam in 1862. Below, a view of Camp Douglas painted by Albert Moyer, of the Pennsylvania Volunteer Infantry, one of the guards. *(Pinkerton Collection.)*

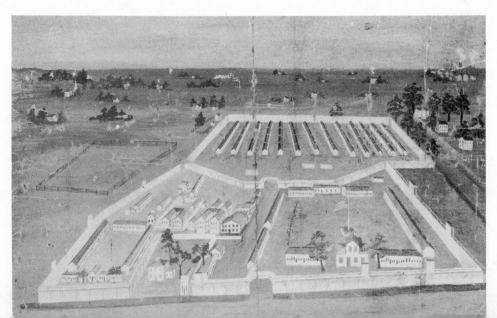

man in Wilbur Fisk Storey, whose *Times* never hesitated to criticize the North. Storey's blasts so infuriated General Ambrose Burnside that on June 2, 1863, he issued an order from his Cincinnati headquarters, suppressing the newspaper. A mob of 20,000, led by the southern gamblers, soon appeared in the streets. Some proposed to burn the *Tribune* in retaliation, but William B. Ogden assembled the saner citizens and sent a plea to President Lincoln, urging that Burnside's order be revoked. This was done, and on June 5, the *Times* resumed publication.

But the criminals continued to swagger as if they owned the town. Their gambling hells and vice dens attracted soldiers on furlough, bounty jumpers, and workers with fat pay envelopes. A renegade called Cap Hyman and another named George Trussell fought for power. Shootings were so frequent that Randolph Street west of State, where the gamblers operated, became known as Hairtrigger Block. Finally Trussell's mistress killed him and Hyman took over. He ruled a kingdom centered about Conley's Patch, at Wells and Monroe streets, where Roger Plant, midget Yorkshireman, had his vicious Under the Willow resort, plus the Randolph Street gambling area.

Soon Hyman provided protection for Carrie Watson's elegant brothel on Clark Street, the seamen's dives on North Wells, and most of the 350 other resorts that roared wide open through the war. When Hyman married Annie Stafford, a leading madam, and extended his domain north by opening a roadhouse in Lake View, leading citizens attended the opening and the guest of honor was Captain Jack Nelson, deputy superintendent of police.

Chicago was in constant dread that the criminals would join forces with the 8,000 Confederate soldiers held in Camp Douglas just south of town. But Washington ignored pleas for additional guards. Trouble was expected when "Peace Democrats" held their 1864 convention in Chicago's public square, a move forced because no citizen would rent them a hall. Clement L. Vallandingham harangued the delegates and Long John Wentworth, again mayor, braved Copperhead wrath to reply. When even Storey refused to back Vallandingham's group, the town breathed a bit more easily.

But on the night before the November election, federal agents swept through the city, rounding up Confederate spies and their Copperhead conspir-

The town's celebration of victory and peace was starkly ended the morning of April 15 when word of the assassination of President Lincoln reached the newspapers. Every business house in the city closed as the people went into mourning. The body of the martyred president arrived May 2 aboard a black-draped Illinois Central funeral train, which waited on a lake-front pier while 40,000 citizens escorted the cortege to the courthouse. *(Illinois Central.)*

ators, whom they accused of a bizarre plot to free the Camp Douglas prisoners, take over Chicago, and stuff the ballot boxes for pro-southern candidates. Chicagoans went nervously to the polls guarded by federal troops and backed Lincoln by a 2,000 majority over General George B. McClellan, nominee of the regular Democrats.

The fall of Richmond on April 3, 1865, sent the town into a wild celebration that continued through the Confederacy's collapse a week later. Then, on April 15, citizens learned of the assassination of President Lincoln the previous day. For the first time every business house in Chicago, including the grogshops, was closed. The grand opening of the magnificent new Crosby Opera House was delayed. On May 2, the body of the president arrived to lie in state in the courthouse. There an estimated 125,000 citizens paid him their last respects.

As the 1860s rushed to a close, Chicago was a rich city, dominant in the West. Its population totaled almost 300,000, nearly triple that at the beginning of the war. Now, finally, St. Louis and Cincinnati were outdistanced. Only New York, Boston, and Philadelphia sold more goods. None packed as much pork and beef, or shipped more grain. The railroads alone earned nearly $49,000,-000 in 1869 as the city's exports rose to $178,-000,000. The expanding business and industrial district spread south and west from the river, its 79 blocks of stores, hotels, and wholesale houses lining new-paved streets. Potter Palmer, grown rich in merchandising and his wartime cotton speculation, had acquired three fourths of a mile along State Street and was converting it to a new street of merchants. His marble palace, leased by Field, Leiter and Company at $50,000 a year, stood at one end, his new Palmer House at the other.

All three divisions of the city were now served by horse-car lines which carried thousands of passengers to the new shopping district. The river was spanned by 27 bridges. To the north, beyond McCormick's $600,000 reaper works, were new mansions of the rich, fronting Pine and Rush streets. Beyond them, the town's new and thriving breweries clustered around the waterworks. West, along the north branch of the river, were distilleries, tanneries, flour mills, and ironworks. West of the south branch of the river stretched 160 acres of iron and brass foundries and small manufactories. South of Van Buren Street were 500 acres of lumberyards and planing mills, extending all the way to Twenty-second and Ashland streets. Farther south, along the river, were new industrial developments, using an estimated 14 miles of docks. The world's biggest stockyards were at Thirty-ninth and Halsted streets, surrounded by packing plants. To the east were the railroad yards, carshops, boiler factories, and bridge and iron plants.

Packed against the expensive residential districts, along Prairie Avenue and the lake front on the south, and all the way to the new Lincoln Park on the north, was a ring of 40,000 frame houses and tenements where dwelt two thirds of the population, close to the plants which gave them work. Rooming houses and shacks lined muddy, unpaved streets which ran with sewage and were littered with dead rats. Most such neighborhoods could be found by the stench alone, said the *Tribune,* as it warned that someday the pine boards and shingles would flare up in a terrible holocaust. Beyond the worst slums to the southwest was Bridgeport, an Irish community. To the north, around Chicago Avenue and State Street, the Swedes had settled. Northwest, on North Avenue, the Germans lived, drank their lager, and read German-language newspapers.

It was a time of easy morals and easy money. Roswell B. Mason, the Illinois Central builder, was in the mayor's chair. The *Tribune* and the *Evening Journal* called him an honest man pre-

From a rare daguerreotype is this reproduction of the somber moment when President Lincoln's funeral cortege approached the north entrance of the courthouse. In the square are ranks of soldiers. *(Chicago Historical Society.)*

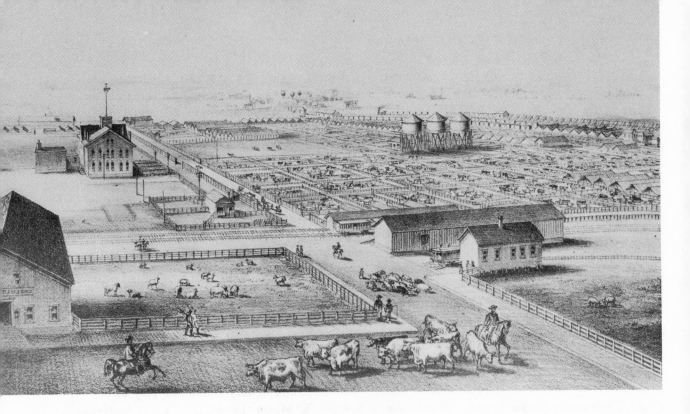

For years Chicago's corn and grain trade was conducted in the streets where farmers parked their wagons, or along the lake front. Cattle were hauled or driven to a half-dozen stockyards, usually situated near one of the plank roads, with a drovers' hotel handy. In 1856, the Board of Trade, first organized in 1848, took rooms of its own and arranged for telegraphic market reports, but the lake front and street trading continued. Membership in the Board of Trade, costing only $5.00, rose from 665 to 1,462 during the war. The scattered stockyards were inefficient and inadequate for the heavy livestock shipments and in 1864 railroads and packers joined to organize The Union Stock Yard and Transit Company. Extensive yards, covering 345 acres, were constructed at Halsted and Thirty-ninth streets. The new yards, biggest and most modern in the world, opened for business on Christmas Day, 1865. *(Chicago Public Library.)*

siding over a den of thieves. Gambling thrived and brothels operated freely. Barrel houses and concert saloons were spread through the town. Councilmen were accused of making fortunes from paving, bridge, and tunnel contracts. Taxes shot up 400 per cent in ten years.

Miss Addie Ballou, of Boston, arrived to speak at Farwell Hall in September 1871, and spent two weeks investigating vice and crime. "It is a deplorable fact that Chicago is an evil place," she declared. "The city fathers and clergymen countenance not only 350 brothels, but hundreds more places of assignation. I have personally seen city officials and ministers in the brothels. Your taxes are going to the support of harlots. It is not only the criminals who maintain vice, but the elite of this city, which has become a modern Sodom that must perish if it does not change its ways!"

Few persons attended the lecture, and some newspapers ignored it. Most citizens preferred the lyrical words of Will Carleton, famed for *Over the Hill to the Poorhouse,* who wrote: "This is the rich and voluptuous city, The beauty-thronged, mansion-decked city, The golden-crowned, glorious Chicago, the Queen of the North and the West."

Chicago was the country's leading horse and mule market during the war, much of the activity centering about Haymarket Square, shown here as it appeared in 1866. (*Chicago Tribune Library.*)

Uranus B. Crosby's $600,000 opera house was built on the north side of Washington Street, near State, in 1865. It opened April 17, with Chicago society attending for the Grau Italian Opera Company's presentation of *Il Trovatore*. Despite its splendor, Crosby's was not a financial success. Several benefit lotteries were organized to support it. Finally the theater itself was given away in a giant lottery in which $900,000 worth of tickets were sold. The winner was said to be A. H. Lee, of Prairie du Rocher, Illinois, who promptly sold the theater back to Crosby for $200,000. Some skeptics publicly doubted the existence of Mr. Lee. (*Newberry Library.*)

General Ulysses S. Grant, northern hero of the Civil War, was nominated for president of the United States by the Republicans on May 28, 1868. An artist here depicts the successful roll call for Grant, climaxing the convention at Crosby's Opera House. *(Chicago Historical Society.)*

A scandal of the times involved Wilbur Fisk Storey, the vitriolic Copperhead editor, who bought the *Chicago Times* from Senator Douglas in 1861 and made it an inflammatory anti-war publication. Storey battled politicians and generals, but met his match when he accused Lydia Thompson, tempestuous star of *The Black Crook* Company, of "capering lasciviously" and implied she was little more than a strumpet. Miss Thompson waylaid the editor near his home and horsewhipped him. The town guffawed at the news. *(Authors' Collection.)*

Two other spirited girls of the time were Tennessee Claflin (left) and her sister, Victoria Woodhull, clairvoyants who later became free-love advocates. They arrived in Chicago in 1866 after being charged with assignation in Cincinnati and murder in Ottawa, Illinois. Tennessee, billed as "the wonder child," conducted séances at 365 Wabash Avenue. When John Bartels threatened to prove she was no child but his wife, the girls paid him $20,000 to keep quiet. In 1870 the pair went to New York, where they became stockbrokers. Victoria later ran for president of the United States. (*Chicago Historical Society.*)

Some of Chicago's excitement is caught in the lithograph below showing "Chicago's Great Railway Station," published as a premium with *Appleton's Journal.* (*Chicago Historical Society.*)

105

In January 1863, Marshall Field (at left) and Levi Z. Leiter formed a partnership with Potter Palmer and took over his prosperous wholesale and retail dry-goods business. Three years later, the firm moved into the elegant marble palace Palmer had built on North State Street, the beginning of its eminence as "the street of merchants." Field, Leiter, and Palmer ultimately became Marshall Field & Company. *(Field Archives.)*

The Lake Street wholesale district, looking east from State, is pictured here (at right) by Otto Jevne and Peter M. Almini, who issued a fine series of lithographs portraying Chicago of 1865. *(Jevne and Almini Print.)*

Samuel Carson and John Pirie (below) founded a chain of dry-goods stores in down-state Illinois in 1854 and opened a Chicago wholesale house at 20 Lake Street during the war. In 1867, with George and Robert Scott and Andrew MacLeish as additional partners, the company launched a retail store at 136 West Lake Street, later moving to 118-120 State Street where the wholesale and retail activities were consolidated. *(Carson Pirie Scott & Co.)*

George M. Pullman built his first railroad sleeping cars in 1858, remodeling two Chicago & Alton coaches at a cost of $2,000. They ran from Chicago to Bloomington, and J. L. Barnes, the conductor, reported he had trouble getting the passengers to take their boots off when they went to bed. Later, Pullman spent $18,239 to build his first Palace car, the ornately furnished Pioneer. He formed a partnership with Andrew Carnegie, incorporating The Pullman Palace Car Company at $100,000 in 1867. *(The Pullman Company.)*

The town turned to enjoyment after the bleak war years. The grounds of the Chicago Sharpshooters' Association, on the lake front, provided a favored recreational area, now a part of Lincoln Park. At the upper right is the Lake View Hotel. The main gate and stables are at the left, with targets in the background. Other lively sports included velocipede riding and baseball on ice skates. *(Chicago Historical Society.)*

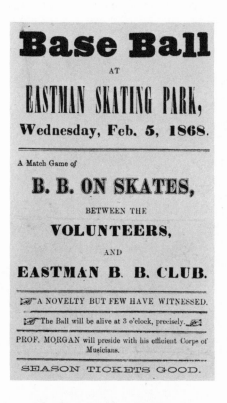

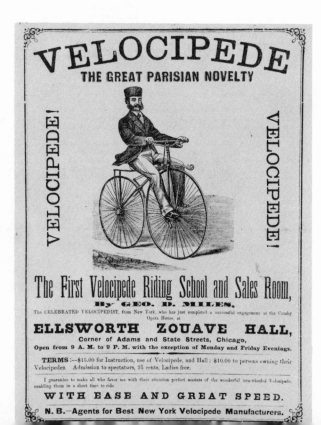

Among the near North Side mansions was this Rush Street home of Leander McCormick, built in 1863. On the steps at left are his son, L. Hamilton McCormick; his wife, their daughter Henrietta; Miss Gilman, the governess; Mrs. Hugh Adams (Amanda McCormick); Leander, and, on the lower steps, Mrs. John Chapman (Mary Adams) and Robert Hall McCormick.

Gay party on Tremont House balcony in 1865. They were honoring George Francis Train, New York author (hat off, sitting). *(Chicago Historical Society.)*

Mayor Ogden, Walter L. Newberry, and George W. Dole were the first to establish fine residences north of the river. Since 1837, Ogden's home at Rush and Ontario was a center where visiting dignitaries, especially those from abroad, were entertained. With the arrival of the McCormicks, Rush Street vied with Terrace Row in wealth and social prestige. The elegant McCormick home was typical of the grand mansions. Above, at right, Robert Hall McCormick appears in the doorway of the parlor, with a view of the back parlor through the door at his left. In the center, the parlor looking toward the high French windows. On the chairs, antimacassars to keep macassar oil used in hair dressing from soiling furniture. At left, the billiard room and bowling alley over the stable, where R. H. McCormick (cue raised) is entertaining friends. *(Chicago Historical Society.)*

From earliest days Chicagoans sought to keep structures from the square at Randolph and Michigan, and the lake-front area immediately east. These lots, they said, were "Chicago's lungs." This view of Dearborn Park is northeast, toward the Pullman Building, and is the site of the Chicago Public Library. In 1869, a park system for each of the three divisions of the city was established, and Lincoln, Garfield, Jackson, and Grant parks were subsequently created. *(Kaufmann & Fabry.)*

Chicagoans and visitors alike ogled the curiosities gathered together by Colonel Joseph H. Wood for his museum on Randolph Street. *(Jevne & Almini.)* Ladies, downtown for the day, took luncheon at the Maison Dorée, the only exclusively female restaurant in town. Set in parklike surroundings at Wabash Avenue and Monroe Street, the Maison Dorée was managed by Mrs. Anne Johnson. The mansion was built in 1844 by Eli B. Williams, a Lake Street merchant. *(Richard Richard Collection.)*

Above. Looking north from the Lake Street Bridge in 1868 toward the area of the original village at Wolf Point. The elevator on the right is near the site of Miller's Tavern of 1834. The ships are berthed near the former location of Wolf Tavern. Across the north branch of the river shown here the first footbridge was built in 1834, not far from Alexander Robinson's Indian store. *(Chicago Historical Society.)* *Below.* Lumber schooners clustered on the Chicago River, overtaxing docks and private wharves and slips. This scene is east from Rush Street in 1869. At the right the freight shed of the Illinois Central Railroad and the Sturgis and Buckingham elevator on the lake front can be seen. Chicago was still a wooden town, consuming most of its immense imports—in 1868 more than a billion and a half board feet. In the yards district, lumber was frequently stacked in piles 30 feet high, lining both sides of the river almost solidly for a distance of nearly two miles south and west of Madison Street. *(Chicago Historical Society.)*

Michigan Avenue was a quiet street of elegant homes and residential hotels in 1871. At Adams and Michigan, in the foreground, is the residence of H. H. Honore, whose daughter, Bertha, married Potter Palmer and became the queen of Chicago society. On north were the homes of Nelson and Henry Tuttle, Henry Farnum, and the marble mansion where William H. Brown had entertained President-elect and Mrs. Lincoln when they were in Chicago for a reception. Many of the streets were tree-lined, supporting the town's motto, *"Urbs in Horto"*—City in a Garden. Most homes and business buildings were of wood. *(Chicago Historical Society.)*

The Great Fire VII

In a strange season, the Chicago wind was hot and crisp on the evening of October 8, 1871.

All that summer the whole Midwest and large patches of the West had been afflicted with drought. Leaves had started dropping as early as July; only one inch of rain had fallen between July and October; on grazing lands livestock by the thousands had perished near arid mudholes. And in these dry months the city had suffered an inordinate number of fires that fed eagerly on its pinewood homes, rickety shanties, and flimsy buildings. In the first week of October alone thirty such blazes had sprung up, the fiercest only the night before on the West Side, a conflagration that involved all of the city's 200 harassed firemen before it finally spent itself in wiping out four square blocks and wreaking $750,000 in damages.

But this fire was merely the harbinger of the disaster, immense and terrible, that befell the city on this Sunday evening.

It began in a small stable behind the frame house of Patrick and Catherine O'Leary at 137 De Koven Street, a muddy tract near Halsted and Twelfth streets. Although flames were seen as early as 9 P.M., it was fully half an hour before an alarm was sounded and the first fire company was dispatched. Persistent lore would attribute the start of this blaze to a lamp upset by the O'Leary cow and setting afire dry hay stored in the barn. But whatever the cause the effects were rapid and calamitous. Swiftly red-black flames streaked out of the structure and soon the wind tore from it burning brands and sticks and sent them hurtling

into other barns and dwellings, all made of quick-burning pine.

Delays, confusion, and downright inefficiency hampered the fire fighters; much of their equipment broke down. They cursed and they raged, but they were powerless against the spreading fire. The dry wind, traveling at 30 miles an hour, did its part in sending flames to the north and to the east. Even worse was a kind of vicious wind whipped up by the fire itself, made of self-generating whirls of flame and heated air—"fire devils" they were later called—that were capable of transporting blazing brands and sparks and masses of flame through the air for almost half a mile.

An hour after the haystack fire in the O'Leary barn began, flames hundreds of yards in width and a hundred feet high were traveling toward the heart of the city. Hour after hour they continued, with nothing seemingly able to stop them; hope that the river would be a natural barrier vanished as the flames leaped across the south branch into the wholesale business district and leveled factories and warehouses. They swept through the wretched cribs and brothels and low dwellings of Conley's Patch. They reached out soon enough for such sumptuous and newly built hotels as the Palmer House and the Grand Pacific, then for the Sherman House and the Tremont House, for the dwellings on Terrace Row as well as the vice districts cluttered near the courthouse. By 1:30 A.M. the courthouse itself was ablaze and within thirty minutes, its mighty bell still clanging as it had done since the fire's first hour, down toppled

The place where the Great Fire began. The frame cottage and stable of Patrick and Catherine O'Leary on De Koven Street as it appeared—unhurt, ironically, by the flames—a week after the disaster. *(Chicago Historical Society.)*

Contemporary sketches of the kind of equipment—some of which broke down—that was used to fight the disastrous blaze. Above is Hose Cart No. 6 and (below) is Steamer No. 17. *(Chicago Historical Society.)*

As the fire spread, thousands of Chicagoans fled from their homes, carrying bundles, boxes, anything else they could lay their hands on. In this on-the-spot drawing, John B. Chapin recorded one crowd of refugees surging across the Randolph Street Bridge. *(Chicago's Great Century.)*

its cupola and much of the famous structure itself.

On every street leading toward the main branch of the river and to the "blessed lake shore" surged the people. There were crazed men and brave ones, noble ones and craven ones. On Lake Street, still a street of merchants, and along Randolph Street, whose bridge, still intact and whole, offered egress to parts as yet untouched by the blaze, the press of men, women, and children was suffocatingly close. They carried boxes and packages, bundles, babies, housewares, toys, picture frames, chairs. They crashed through fences and ripped down awnings. Some yelled and some plodded along silently. Some pushed their way down the street and some were shoved and trampled. And here and there could be seen a man or woman, eyes glazed and faces streaked with smoke grime, crying out, "Chicago is doomed! God has punished us all!" On other streets leading away from the center of the fire were men with coaches, omnibuses, and wagons; they offered to carry anyone who could pay—$150 was the asking price—toward the lake shore or over the river bridges to the city limits beyond Lincoln Park; some of these men were honest, but some were dastards, ready in an instant to dump their passengers if others offered more money.

There were looting and widespread thievery.

In some sectors the hordes were able to get to the river and fight their way to boats docked there. This photograph, though it seems unusually realistic, actually was made of a portion of the famous cycloramic reproduction of the fire that was a popular attraction in Chicago in the mid-1870's. (*Gross Cyclorama.*)

Even while flames streaked through department stores on State Street and Wabash Avenue, vandals broke in and left with bolts of cloth, suits, silks, dresses. A block from Field, Leiter and Company, where Marshall Field and his associates had fought in vain to save their "Marble Palace," men and women stomped along the streets through stacks of oil paintings, books, musical instruments, mirrors, glassware. From the windows of dry-goods stores thieves hurled silks and fabrics to accomplices on the crackling sidewalks. Mayor Mason had already issued the first of many emergency proclamations, ordering all saloons to close; there was little need for such precautions now, for already many of the drinking places in the burning sections had been invaded by looters who smashed bottles and guzzled liquor and overturned whisky barrels. Not only stores but private homes

were broken into; on Terrace Row, Deacon Bross came upon a rascal fleeing from his half-demolished house and wearing half-a-dozen of his suits. The beetle-browed Bross made only a perfunctory move to stop the thief, saying resignedly, "Well, go along, you might as well have them as let them burn." Down State Street's cobblestones staggered a woman, her scrawny arms laden with stolen dresses and finery, and over and over again she shrilled, "Chickey chickey craney crow! I went to the well to wash my toe!" And at the foot of the Clark Street bridge sprawled a boy, dead beneath a marble slab; on his hands were two white kid gloves and in his pockets were stuffed dozens of gold-plated sleeve buttons.

Many men kept their heads amid all the frenzy. At the Field and Leiter store, the two partners, while others continued to pour water into fires

Right. C. S. Reinhart, one of the staff dispatched immediately by *Harper's Weekly* to cover the historic fire, drew this group of refugees for the magazine's cover of October 28, 1871. *(Harper's Weekly.)*

Below. In the same issue of the famous magazine appeared this graphic drawing by an unnamed artist of refugees streaming past Potter's Field on the outskirts of Lincoln Park at the northern limits of the fire. *(Harper's Weekly.)*

A vivid panoramic view of the destruction as seen from north of Congress Street after the flames subsided. Drawn from photographs made by Thomas S. Sweeney, the various numbered locations and landmarks are: 1, Standard Club; 2, Congress Hall; 3, railroad depot; 4, Chapel of the First Presbyterian Church; 5, Congress Street; 6, First Presbyterian Church; 7, State Street; 8, Grand Pacific Hotel; 9, Wabash Avenue; 10, Bigelow Hotel; 11, Honore Block; 12, St. Paul's; 13, Customhouse and Post Office; 14, *Tribune* and *Evening Post;* 15, First National Bank; 16, Booksellers' Row; 17, Trinity Methodist Episcopal Church; 18, Catholic Bishop's Palace; 19, Chicago Club; 20, Illinois Central Depot; 21, Elevator B.; 22, Michigan Avenue; 23, Lake Michigan; 24, Terrace Row; 25, J. Y. Scammon's home. *(Harper's Weekly.)*

Right. "Far and wide the ruins lay," wrote one lyricist about the effects of the fire. This was all that remained of a grand office building on Washington Street. *(Chicago Sun-Times Library.)*

Left. Long after the Great Fire was over, books, pamphlets, and songs were written about it, lectures with illustrated slides were well attended, and photographers with stereopticon views and before-and-after cards thrived. Here is one such card, showing the courthouse and city hall. *(Chicago Public Library.)*

that sprouted everywhere, ordered much of their merchandise taken first to the lake shore and later, to thwart vandals, to a fire-free area near Leiter's mansion on Prairie Avenue. And in the precious minutes before the flames reached the new Palmer House, its builder, John Mills Van Osdel, Chicago's pioneer architect, gathered together all his construction plans and record books, went to the hotel's basement and dug a pit into which he placed all the documents; he covered the hole with two feet of sand and a thick layer of damp clay, thereby not only saving the important blueprints and other papers from destruction but devising, in this impromptu way, a method of fireproofing with clay tile that would be extensively used for years to come. Lambert Tree, distinguished lawyer of the era and later an equally distinguished diplomat, walked calmly from his home on the North Side to his law office at Dearborn and Washington streets, gathered his papers, and returned on foot by way of the burning Rush Street Bridge. Theodore Thomas, fully two decades away from becoming a permanent Chicagoan, was in town for a concert with his orchestra; he called his musicians together in their quarters at the St. James Hotel and cool-headedly directed them to gather

instruments and belongings, then led them to safety.

But panic and fear prevailed in most places, especially when the fire, in the early-morning hours of the second day of its destructive lifetime, showed scant signs of slackening and continued on its northerly route. Like a swaggering conqueror, it made its destructive way in the areas extending from the north side of the river. Warehouses on the banks flared up and toppled, their sparks flicking the ships docked nearby or being borne ever northward by the "fire devils." The huge McCormick Works at Pine Street fell victim as easily as did the reaper magnate's mansion on Rush Street. Half a mile north of the river the waterworks and adjoining stone water tower were set aflame and appeared—mistakenly, as it happily turned out—to be heading for certain doom. Other mansions met a fate similar to that of McCormick's. In a spacious, parklike block bounded by Rush, Erie, Pine, and Ontario streets and adorned with elm trees and garnished with grapevines and Virginia creeper growing over arbors and trellises, stood the home of Isaac Newton Arnold, important lawyer, bibliophile, and art collector. Fiercely he and his family and servants

The day before the Great Fire the roof of the spanking-new Grand Pacific Hotel at Clark and Jackson streets was about to be laid. It never was. All that was left of the imposing inn is seen in this stereopticon view taken by one of the city's photographers of that day. *(J. Carbutt.)*

Above. "Dante's Inferno" is what this awesome sight of the burned-out commercial district reminded those who saw the reproduction in the famous cyclorama. In this sector alone nearly 4,000 buildings were destroyed. *(Gross Cyclorama.)*

Below. Among the many edifices that were devastated by the flames was the Second Presbyterian Church. *(Chicago Historical Society.)*

strove to save his $250,000 house and its inestimable treasures and furnishings. But the city pumps had given out, and Arnold trudged along with other refugees heading for the lake shore. Beyond him, throngs pushed into Lincoln Park past cemeteries whose wooden headstones had burned or whose stone vaults had cracked open to reveal their skeletons. All that was later found intact on Arnold's burned-out lawn was a smoke-blackened dial whose inscription, in Latin, read: "I number none but serene hours." Arnold's home was of solid brick, as were the similarly expensive and similarly demolished mansions of his rich neighbors; one of the historic fire's freakish events was that a rare survivor in this area—indeed, in all of the fire-ravaged sectors—was the home of Mahlon D. Ogden, just north of Washington Square, a large and roomy edifice built almost entirely of wood.

Finally, the Great Fire seemed to halt as if of its own choosing, as if weary of having spent all

Stark symbol of the fire's devastation was this section of one of the many buildings near the courthouse, whose bell clanged the city's fate until it tumbled with the walls early on the fire's first morning. (*Chicago Sun-Times Library.*)

its awesome fury. By late Monday afternoon it began to taper off near the city limits at Fullerton Avenue and to subside, and that night, some twenty-seven hours after the first spurts of flame had leaped out of the O'Leary barn, rain fell and continued for an hour or more. The worst calamity in the city's lifetime was over. On the dismal Tuesday morning of October 11 the citizens stared at the havoc.

Completely destroyed was an area of three and a half square miles in which had stood 18,000 homes, stores, hotels, bridges, churches, manufacturing establishments, railroad stations, government buildings. The full property loss came to $200,000,000 and the known dead were 250, with as many or more never accounted for. The number of homeless was at least 100,000. Gone was the entire business district, except for the partially completed Nixon Building at La Salle and Monroe streets—which was duly finished and as

quickly dubbed by its owners "Chicago's First Fireproof Building"—and the Lind Block at Market and Randolph streets. For the rest, the area was a mass of twisted girders, fallen columns of iron and of stone, vast piles of bricks and rocks and cornices—everywhere the kind of desolation that reminded observers of cities that had been inundated by hot lava. And in some sectors of the devastated areas were strange sights: a row of dwellings untouched yet completely surrounded by whole blocks completely ruined; church towers noble and intact and looming high above gutted buildings and fallen walls; and, as a final irony, the O'Leary barn and house virtually whole in a patch of land that looked as if the contents of some vast cauldron had been spilled on it.

The populace stared and gasped, and some prepared at once to leave the city forever, and some called the tragedy God's vengeance on a sinful community, and some thought instantly of re-

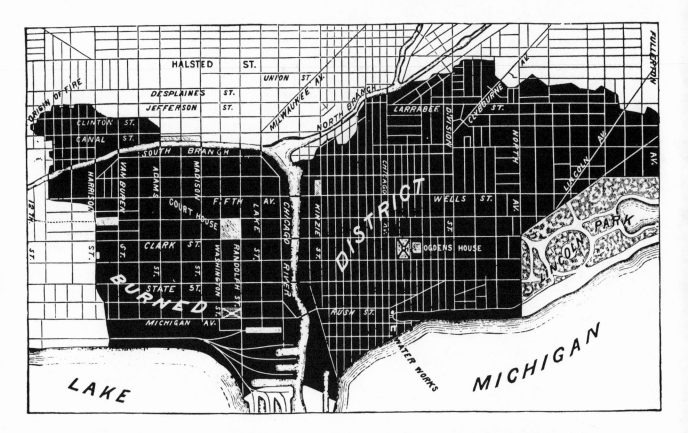

Above. The fire's toll: $200,000,000 in property damage, 250 lives counted lost and as many or more unaccounted for, 17,450 buildings destroyed, three-and-one-half square miles of blackened ruins. *(Chicago Municipal Reference Library.)*

Right. This was one of several proclamations issued by Mayor Mason. One of his earliest, in the hours immediately after the fire started, was to ban the sale of liquor "in consequence of the great calamity that has befallen our city and for the preservation of good order." *(Chicago Municipal Reference Library.)*

PROCLAMATION!

The preservation of the good order and peace of the city is hereby entrusted to Lieut. General P. H. Sheridan, U. S. Army.

The Police will act in conjunction with the Lieut. General in the preservation of the peace and quiet of the city, and the Superintendent of Police will consult with him to that end.

The intent hereof being to preserve the peace of the city, without interfering with the functions of the City Government.

Given under my hand this 11th day of October, 1871.

R. B. MASON, Mayor.

First to establish themselves in the business district was the firm of Shock, Bigford and Company. Several alert young men found an old mahogany sideboard at State and Harrison streets and bought it and a barrel and some glasses for only $2.50. They set it up at 169 South Dearborn Street, opposite the ruins of the old post office, and sold cigars, tobacco, grapes, apples, and cider. *(Joseph Kirkland.)*

generation and recovery. To prevent more looting —on the day after the fire ceased, hordes of criminals from surrounding cities trooped into town intent on brigandage—Mayor Mason issued a proclamation shifting all police powers to General Philip Sheridan, commanding the local division of the War Department. "Little Phil" had tried, valiantly if unsuccessfully, to balk the spread of the fire by blowing up buildings in the path of the flames. He now took his additional duties seriously and helped to quell the activities of vandals and pillagers, although Mayor Mason's action evoked from Governor John Palmer official protests about federal encroachment on local authority.

And again the Boosters and the Boomers were ready with estimates and prophecies. On the morning after the fire, John Stephen Wright walked slowly amid the ashes and ruins of Wabash Avenue. At the corner of Congress Street he met D. H. Horton, the publisher of his many books extolling an earlier Chicago. "Well, Wright," asked Horton, "what do you think now of the future of Chicago?"

Solemnly the old man answered: "I will tell you what it is. Chicago will have more men, more money, more business within five years than she would have had without the fire."

Such feelings were reflected in Joseph Medill's *Tribune* with an editorial, on the Wednesday after the fire, shouting:

CHEER UP!

In the midst of a calamity without parallel in the world's history, looking upon the ashes of thirty years' accumulations, the people of this once beautiful city have resolved that CHICAGO SHALL RISE AGAIN!

In Medill's newspapers and in others, on that day and for weeks to come, appeared brave advertisements from merchants large and small: "We Still Live!" and "Resumed Business!" and "Keep the Ball Rolling!" And other notices from stores that sprang up to sell salvaged goods: "No Advantage Taken of the Calamity!"

Medill's sentiments were also echoed by George Frederick Root, the nation's popular song writer, whose hastily written composition, "From the Ruins Our City Shall Rise!" cried out:

Above. Another of the quick-recovery businessmen was William D. Kerfoot, a real-estate dealer whose shack, which he and his friends are seen building here, was the origin of the city's Kerfoot Block. The sign he nailed to the top of the makeshift office became part of Chicago's proud lore: "All Gone but Wife, Children, and ENERGY." (*Harper's Weekly.*)

Below. In the ruins of the First National Bank this man found a safe which he cooled off with pails of water. Of all the banks in the city, only one survived the fire; for the others, the losses totaled over $1,000,000. (*A. T. Andreas.*)

Above. Harper's Weekly artists and reporters stayed on for weeks following the fire to record the swift resumption of life and business. Theodore R. Davis made this sketch of men and women building temporary shanties on the near North Side. *(Harper's Weekly.) Below.* By a freak, one of the few houses left standing in any stricken area was that of Mahlon D. Ogden, across from the near North Side's Washington Square. Interestingly, ironically, it was made completely of wood while mansions in the surrounding territory that crumbled were of more solid substances. This dwelling was later torn down to make way for the distinguished Newberry Library. *(Chicago Historical Society.)*

Then—and now—the symbol of the city's incredible tragedy and astounding recovery was the water tower a mile north of the river, seen here as one of the rare surviving structures in this haunting photograph taken a day after the Great Fire burned itself out. *(Chicago Historical Society.)*

129

Ruins! Ruins! Far and wide
From the river and lake to the prairie side.
    Dreary, dreary, the darkness falls,
While the autumn winds moan through blackened
        walls.
    But see! The bright rift in the cloud
    And hear the great voice from the shore!
    Our city shall rise!
    Yes, she shall rise!
Queen of the west once more!

Loudest and most strident of all the Boosters at this dire moment was Deacon Bross.

While the city was still smoking he headed toward the East. As the first available eyewitness to the conflagration, he was accosted by reporters, and to each interviewer he gave graphic details that comprised one of the most vivid accounts of the Great Fire. More important, however, for the city's fate and its future were his messages, clear and loud, to eastern bankers, industrialists, workers, office clerks, and anyone within range of his booming voice.

"Go to Chicago now!" he cried. "Young men, hurry there! Old men, send your sons! Women, send your husbands! You will never again have such a chance to make money!"

The Great Fire, he declared, had made it possible for just about everyone to start even in Chicago in the race for fortune. "Now is the time to strike! A delay of a year or two will give an immense advantage to those who start at once. . . . The fire has leveled nearly all distinctions!"

And being a Booster, Deacon Bross was inevitably a prophet. "I tell you," he declaimed, "within five years Chicago's business houses will be rebuilt, and by the year 1900 the new Chicago will boast a population of a million souls. You ask me why? Because I know the Northwest and the vast resources of the broad acres. I know that the location of Chicago makes her the center of this wealthy region and the market for all its products.

"What Chicago has been in the past, she must become in the future—and a hundredfold more! She has only to wait a few short years for the sure development of her manifest destiny!"

Left. The Nixon Block at La Salle and Monroe streets was touted for years as "the only structure in the Chicago Burnt District not damaged by flames." Only partially finished, its floor surfacing and wood trim actually were consumed by the flames, yet the damage was so slight that the building was rushed to completion one week after the fire and served for decades as an office building for architects and businessmen. *(Land Owner Magazine.)*

Midland Metropolis

VIII

The resurgence predicted by Bross and Wright started swiftly and eagerly and continued at a frenetic pace.

There was help and there were funds from other cities and from other lands. Carloads of food and clothing were brought in free of charge by every railroad whose tracks stretched into Chicago. From such a bitter trade rival as St. Louis came $500,000, and with $160,000 from Cincinnati touched off a fund drive that eventually yielded more than $4,000,000 in contributions from the United States and Europe. The Illinois legislature, despite the traditional hostility of its downstate members toward Chicago, appropriated $3,000,000 to help the stricken city rebuild eight bridges and three viaducts destroyed by flames. And from Queen Victoria and her subjects came 8,000 books to serve as the nucleus for the city's first public library.

Above all, most Chicagoans of great and little repute helped themselves. Forty thousand departed after the tragedy but those who remained —and were joined by thousands of others who took Bross's advice—refused to succumb to their misfortunes or to self-pity. Everywhere plans for construction were quickened and intensified. Within a week after the tragedy nearly 6,000 temporary structures were up, many of them stretching along Michigan Avenue to serve varied business enterprises. Marshall Field and Levi Leiter led the merchants of the city in a quick revival of trade; in a horse barn at State and Twentieth streets they set up temporary quarters, opening for business only two weeks after flames had

devoured their handsome Marble Palace. John V. Farwell shifted his wholesale house from Lake Street to Franklin Street, and the Mandel brothers, Leon, Emanuel, and Simon, set up their merchandise establishment at Michigan Avenue and Twenty-second Street. The city's banks had been savagely hit; of 28 national and state institutions, only one remained. But W. F. Coolbaugh, president of the Union National, quickly formed a committee, held meetings, and made arrangements for business to resume; on the Friday after the fire twelve banks were prepared to pay depositors 15 per cent, and in four more days all stood ready to make unconditional payments. Real-estate men and commercial leaders were quick to set up shop once more; a young real-estate man, William D. Kerfoot, achieved inevitable immortality in the city's history by knocking together a wooden shack to serve as an office and topping this cubicle with a sign reading: "All gone but wife, children, and ENERGY."

Joseph Medill ran for mayor in November on a "fireproof" ticket and won handily, urging in his inaugural speech a horde of measures designed to prevent a recurrence of such a major catastrophe. Ordinances duly passed in the City Council tightened safety regulations: no false fronts, greater emphasis on such fire-resistant materials as brick, stone, and iron, an improved water system. Some buildings that were now rising were based on plans drawn before the fire; the first of these, finished in mid-December, was the Central Union Block at the corner of Madison and Market streets, near the site where Field and Leiter planned to estab-

131

Above. Temporary quarters of the city administration were established around the water tank of the waterworks department at Adams and La Salle streets. The tank also served another purpose: in it were stored some 8,000 books sent to the city from Queen Victoria and her subjects, a bounty that served as the start of the city's first public library in 1872. *(Chicago Historical Society.) Below.* Less than a week after the fire, 6,000 temporary business structures had been put up, one stretch of them, shown here, along Michigan Avenue between Jackson and Adams streets. *(J. Carbutt.) Right.* One of the first hotels built—or rebuilt—after the fire was the Grand Pacific at Clark and Jackson streets. Its dining room was the first to display flowers on the tables. *(A. T. Andreas.)*

lish a new store before their eventual move back to State Street. This was not yet the age of architecture of distinction; masons and construction men designed most of the structures in the few years after the fire, although such an expert as John Mills Van Osdel, before proceeding with the new Palmer House, was traveling in Europe and studying styles and techniques. And some unscrupulous and careless builders, adept at evading technicalities in the building regulations, were back at the practice of erecting wooden housing, while others advertising "all-brick buildings" actually were fashioning structures made of wood except for their exterior walls. Little if any action was taken against these miscreants—Medill's *Tribune* warned them angrily of the danger of another fire—for the need for housing was intense. So more and more buildings were put up until in October 1872 the statisticians had these figures to offer: on the South Side, $34,000,000 in new construction; on the North Side, $3,848,500, and on the West Side, $1,893,000. On streets only a few months ago denuded of trees saplings now grew, and where once there had been only ashes and rubble there was spotted, here and there, a patch of green park.

Impatient for the acclaim of others, Chicagoans gathered on that October 30 in a West Side park to lay the cornerstone of a monument as a reminder not only of the fire itself but of "the glorious resurrection which so quickly followed" and to record "the triumph of energy and enterprise, an example worthy of emulation to the end of time." The monument itself was never finished, but the spirit that motivated it did not lag. All the next year recovery continued as energetically as it had in the first year after the fire. Up went the new Grand Pacific Hotel, first of the new Big Four; soon to follow were J. Irving Pearce's Sherman House, and the Tremont House, and, by 1875, the

Palmer House, revolutionary for its time with large rooms, a dining hall of magnificent proportions, and a barbershop famed equally for its service and the silver dollars imbedded in the floor. On the east side of Michigan Avenue near Adams Street was built the Interstate Industrial Exposition Building, a fancy structure of glass and iron designed to lure visitors this year and for many years to see the evidence of the material and cultural progress of Chicago and its environs. This year also saw the building of some $30,000,000 worth of new theaters, railroad stations, banks, office buildings, churches, mansions on the South Side and on the North Side, all this despite the financial panic that afflicted the nation. "This is a peerless metropolis," exulted Andrew Schuman in the *Lakeside Monthly,* asserting that Chicago had proved itself such "in its indomitability of spirit, in its solidity of structure, in its imposing architecture, in its development of a sleepless vitality,

an unaltering faith and an irrepressible progressive impulse."

Beyond such faith and vitality and progressive impulse were some decidedly tangible reasons that spurred the amazing recovery. Not all the city's industries had vanished in the conflagration; unaffected had been 74 per cent of its grain stores, 80 per cent of its lumberyards, and 600 factories, many machine shops, and rolling mills that lay outside the stricken area. Even more important, the fire had not even touched one of the city's prime assets—the Union Stockyards. Such material circumstances had done much to maintain the city's financial credit and essential stability.

Consequently, there was great activity in the Union Stockyards and at the grain elevators in the two vital years after the fire. Throughout 1872 there rolled into the Halsted Street yards twice as many hogs as had arrived in 1870; and in 1873

Left. Another of the Big Four was the Palmer House, which opened in 1875 on the site of the one destroyed in the Great Fire. Its rooms were unusually large and the hotel itself was adorned with tessellated marble and gold trimmings. *(Fred C. Townsend.)*
Above. The elegant grand parlor of the Palmer House. This hotel and the others also had lavish dining rooms where the cuisine was heavy and elaborate. Courses included broiled meats ranging from fowl to ·buffalo, antelope, bear, and mountain sheep, and the best of them featured boned quail in plumage, partridge in nest prairie, blackbirds, and other "ornamental dishes." *(Fred C. Townsend.)*

Right. World famed was the Palmer House Barbershop, with silver dollars imbedded in its floor. Along with the Palmer House and the Grand Pacific, the other chief hotels in the immediate post-fire years were the Tremont, rendezvous for theatrical folk, and the Sherman, which attracted the sporting element. *(Chicago Tribune Library.)*

Philip Danforth Armour made millions in livestock and grain. (*Chicago Sun-Times Library.*)

Gustavus F. Swift went from cattle buyer to innovator of "dressed beef." (*Chicago Tribune Library.*)

Nelson Morris, the third of the packing industry's Big Three in the 1870s. (*Chicago Public Library.*)

the amount of grain was one and a half times the amount that had been shipped in 1869. All this bounty came into the city over twice as many rails as had been constructed in the entire decade before 1871. Annually these totals continued to soar, so that by 1875 Chicago would bypass St. Louis, led by such magnates as Nelson Morris, Gustavus F. Swift, and Philip Danforth Armour —the industry's Big Three—who developed new methods of slaughtering hogs and cattle and of packing pork and beef. The market was not only America but Europe as well, where meat packed as the Chicagoans did it—in dry salt and refrigerated—was far preferable to that packed in the old way, in brine.

Because so much of its economy was based on livestock and grain, Chicago, more than other big cities, was able better to withstand the depression that was touched off late in 1873 with the downfall in New York of Jay Cooke and Company, the country's most influential banking house. Cooke's ruin climaxed months of excessive speculation everywhere in railroads, and bankers in New York, Boston, and Philadelphia now halted cash-

ing of large checks. In Chicago, Lyman J. Gage and other banking associates rallied and continued to pay cash, although there was a tightening of credit and runs on some banks did occur.

Chicago was by no means completely unaffected by the massive letdown in business and industry. There were unemployment and growing unrest, with some plants shutting down completely and others cutting salaries and laying off workers. It was the familiar pattern established in previous panics, except that now the city contained more people, the increase stemming primarily from the influx of immigrants in the post-fire months; and the division between wealth and poverty was sharpened.

All through 1873 and in the many months that followed there were feverish meetings at street corners where speakers railed against "Railroad Kings," and there were grim parades of the unemployed to the city hall and petitions for an eight-hour day and riots and clashes. The newspapers cried "Red Commune!" and industrialists vowed that an eight-hour day would ruin them. All this came to a violent climax in the hot sum-

136

mer of 1877 when thousands of railroad workers, bitter over additional wage cuts, went on strike. Hoodlums and ruffians joined both sides and looted and destroyed property; some businessmen, convinced that revolution was at hand, closed their houses, and the newspapers clamored: "TERROR'S REIGN!" For nearly a week fights and riots raged in the streets. By July 28, the fury subsided; 13 men had been killed and dozens wounded, the loss in livestock and produce was set at $2,400,000 and of the wholesalers at $3,000,000, and impetus had been given to agitation that would have a terrifying climax a decade later.

As the city recovered from the depression, a new figure strode into prominence. Carter Henry

Harrison had arrived in Chicago in 1855 after traveling from his native Kentucky to the capitals of Europe. A large man, handsome and gregarious, he viewed the bustling city of that time and at once claimed it as "my bride." He served in Congress from 1874 to 1878, but his talents, he felt, were more executive than legislative. An advocate of labor unions and civic progress, a man with a sure gift for arousing the affection of the masses, Harrison ran for mayor in 1879 on the Democratic ticket, supported, too, by progressive labor leaders, a circumstance that promptly persuaded some of the newspapers that Harrison was "communistic."

"Our Carter" and "The Eagle" were the names by which Harrison was fondly called. He de-

The Union Stockyards, the center of the city's Packingtown from its first years. Upton Sinclair's later writings about it and its people in *The Jungle* brought reforms. Sarah Bernhardt viewed the yards on a visit to the city and said they were "a dreadful and magnificent sight." *(Chicago Public Library.)*

At each Industrial Exposition, souvenir books were sold, itemizing all exhibits and attractions. For one of them the Chicago and Alton Railroad prepared this detail-crammed display cover to illustrate its special cars that ran between Chicago and Kansas City and St. Louis: "The only line running a sufficient number of reclining chair cars to accommodate all its patrons." *(Chicago Public Library.)*

Left. To signalize the city's recovery, there was built on Michigan Avenue near Adams this Interstate Industrial Exposition Building. For nearly two decades after 1873, fairs were held here to show the material advancements of Chicago and its Midwest neighbors; Theodore Thomas presented his orchestra in annual seasonal concerts; opera companies offered their productions. The building, which Chicagoans liked to think of as their "Crystal Palace," also served as temporary quarters for Field, Leiter and Company when they were burned out in a massive fire in 1874. It was torn down at the end of 1891 to make way for the present Art Institute of Chicago. *(Kaufmann-Fabry.)*

Below. The Panic of 1873, though less virulent in Chicago than in other major cities, nevertheless brought with it unemployment and struggles between labor and capital. When railroad workers went out on strike, troops were summoned fresh from the Indian campaigns. There were scores of conflicts between soldiers and strikers, mostly around the viaducts at South Halsted Street, of which this is a contemporary illustration. *(Anarchy and Anarchists.)*

lighted in donning silk underwear and well-cut clothes and marching off to his favorite eating place, Billy Boyle's Chop House, to lunch sumptuously and eat his favorite food, watermelon; he doted even more on settling his 225-pound frame on his chestnut-brown horse to gallop all over his city, waving his inevitable black slouch hat to bystanders or dismounting to hold earnest conversations with anyone offering suggestions for civic improvement. Although the newspapers opposed him in and out of office, they and his other critics were compelled to admit he was an honest man, despite the perennial rumor that part of his support came from Michael Cassius "King Mike" McDonald, czar of the city's gambling districts. The populace adored "Our Carter" and would return him to his office four more times.

An advocate of the "Live and Let Live" philosophy, Harrison ran a wide-open town. He was skeptical of attempts to legislate morality, and although he listened resignedly to reports from committees of reformers he believed that such sins as prostitution and gambling were too ingrained in society's ways to eradicate by law. So there were pleasures aplenty in the Harrison era that stretched, in its first phase, from 1879 to 1887, and some were considered illicit and some were joys of clearer hue. Harrison loved to brag about his city—"Its streets are lined with business houses and residences vying in splendor with the palaces of princes and nobles in other lands"—but his boasts were not empty ones. Chicago was indeed a city of substantial homes and industries in these years, and it was the locale, too, of some of the

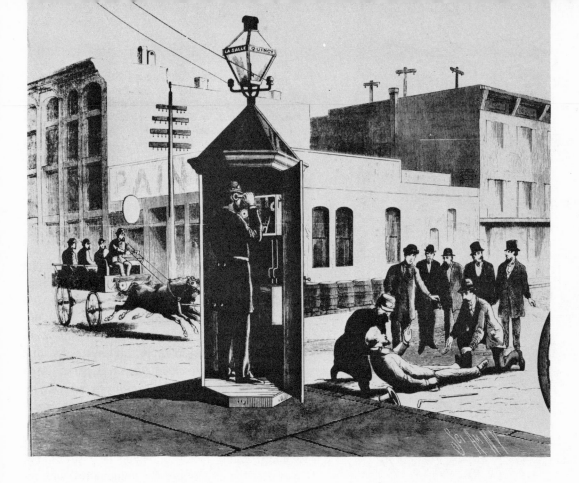

Above. Chicago was the first city in the world to adopt, in 1880, the telephone for police patrol work. This picture, which first appeared in the *Scientific American,* purported to show such an alarm box at La Salle and Quincy streets. The boxes were large enough to hold only a single man; some policemen used them to steal naps, piling up clean cedar paving blocks for use as easy chairs. *(Illinois Bell Telephone Company.)*

"A Flurry in Wheat" this drawing of activity in the Board of Trade—"The Pit"—was titled, illustrating *Harper's* account of Chicago's prowess as a grain center in 1880. In that year the city was without a peer as a primary transfer market, receiving more than two and a half times as much grain and flour as her nearest competitor, St. Louis. In time of financial panic, the sale of grain gave Chicago a quick currency. *(Harper's New Monthly Magazine.)*

Kinsley's Restaurant on Adams Street was one of many fine eating places in the bounteous Harrison era. Others included Rector's, which had, besides a fanciful cuisine, a goldfish aquarium; Billy Boyle's Chop House, meeting place for politicians; the Boston Oyster House, and Chapin and Gore's, where famous sports figures and actors gathered. *(Chicago Historical Society.)*

finest restaurants in the land and of good saloons (Harrison permitted them to stay open on Sundays) and of cultural events at Central Music Hall and of sporting attractions at the new Washington Park Race Track. Supplying substance to Harrison's boosterism were improvements that ranged from an expanded system of parks to the replacement in 1882 of horse-drawn vehicles by the newfangled cable cars, first on State Street and soon as far south as Jackson Park.

There were bountiful increases everywhere: schools, clubs, factories, telephones, stores, bequests to the city by pioneer millionaires, and, inevitably, population. And there were visitors, as always come to see how true were the things they had heard and read: strong farm boys, adventurous young men from the East, famous personages such as the dandified British writer, Oscar Wilde, and the famed French actress, Sarah Bernhardt. Wilde, lounging in his suite at the Grand Pacific Hotel, told reporters that Chicago society was mildly passable but the city itself was "too dreary for me" and its famous water tower "a castellated monstrosity with pepperboxes stuck all over it." The divine Sarah remembered the city forevermore as one "in which men pass each other without ever stopping, with knitted brows, with one thought in mind: the end to attain."

In the final year of Harrison's fourth term there occurred a major tragedy that focused the world's attention on the city.

Ever since 1877, Chicago had been a center of strife between labor and capital. Among the ranks of both were extremists: radicals and anarchists who cried that dynamite was the workingman's best means of obtaining justice, and industrialists

Above. The first American derby was run in Chicago's Washington Park in 1884, won by Modesto. For years Washington Park was one of the city's sumptuous racing clubs, attracting both the gamblers and the society leaders, who made their trips to the race track gay events, driving in processions of polished carriages and tallyhos down Michigan Avenue to the South Side racing course. *(Chicago Sun-Times Library.)*

Right. Chicago's women—those who could afford to —patronized such shops as the millinery establishment shown here. In society circles there was a "New Woman," setting the styles and modes, living in homes that were usually garish monstrosities modeled after French mansions. The New Woman insisted she was an exponent of "taste" and this, in the 1880s, mean that she doted on gilt chairs and horsehair sofas, bought her chignons and Lily Langtry bangs at Campbell's Hair Store, wore the American Elastic Bosom if her form lacked proper roundness, and listed in the Bon-Ton Directory her hours for receiving guests. *(Chicago Tribune Library.)*

Charles F. Gunther was an alderman, owner of one of the most popular ice-cream parlors, and an inveterate hobbyist and collector. Mostly through his efforts Libby Prison was transported stone by stone from Richmond and rebuilt on Wabash Avenue south of Twelfth Street as a Civil War Museum. Later it was replaced by the Coliseum, a stadium where civic celebrations, balls, and political conventions were held. *(Chicago Historical Society.)*

Indoor swimming was a popular sport and there were a number of natatoriums to serve the customers. This is a drawing of one of the most popular, Kadish's, at Jackson Street and Michigan Avenue. *(Chicago Historical Society.)*

"A Chicago Omnibus." Actually, such transportation was a rare sight in the early 1880s. Horsecars had served the city since 1859 and they and these little bobtailed cars were about to make way now for a new-fangled kind of transportation: the cable car. *(Scribner's Monthly.)* Below is one of the first used in the city. Cable cars were introduced on State Street in 1882 and amazed the citizenry by running twenty blocks in thirty-one minutes. *(Chicago Transit Authority.)*

Above. The circular that summoned the populace to the fateful meeting of May 4, 1886, in Haymarket Square. *(Chicago Sun-Times Library.)*

Above Right. A contemporary painting of the precipitous moment in Haymarket Square. Samuel Fielden, an anarchist known as "Good-natured Sam," was addressing the crowd when Captain William Ward advanced at the head of a force of policemen from the Desplaines Street Station. "In the name of the people of the state of Illinois!" shouted Ward, "I command you to disperse!" Replied Fielden: "We are peaceable!" *(Century Magazine.)*

who advocated public lynchings of anyone who dared speak against them. Foremost in the radical ranks were Albert R. Parsons, a writer, Confederate Army veteran, and leader in the Central Labor Union, a combine of left-wing trade-unions, and August Spies, fiery-tongued editor of the *Arbeiter Zeitung,* a German workers' newspaper.

Mounting unemployment since 1884 had led to new demands for public works, the eight-hour day, and, from anarchistic quarters, revision of the economic system. By May 1886, 58,000 workers were on strike in the city. On May 3, there was a clash between workers and Pinkerton police and special guards at the strike-bound McCormick Harvester Works on Blue Island Avenue. Shots had been fired into the crowd, killing one and wounding many.

Above. Just as Fielden replied, someone threw a bomb into the ranks of the police. They fell dead and dying; others opened fire on the crowd. A roundup of all anarchists and left-wingers and even moderates was instantly ordered by police officials. (*Anarchy and Anarchists.*)

The man who led the intensive hunt for the Haymarket Square anarchists was Police Captain Michael Schaack. His search and free-ranging, wholesale roundups finally turned up eight men whom police charged with murder. (*Authors' Collection.*)

Spies hurried to his newspaper and penned a bitter circular calling for "Revenge!" and a mass protest meeting the following night. Some 2,000 persons responded, gathering in a peevish drizzle at Haymarket Square on Desplaines Street off Randolph Street. One orator after another spoke, excoriating the police, strikebreakers, bosses. But beyond occasional booing and hissing nothing untoward happened; even Harrison himself, come to watch, walked off, certain the meeting would fizzle out peacefully.

But when Inspector John Bonfield at the nearby Desplaines Street Station heard of what was being said at the meeting, he dispatched Captain William Ward there with 176 policemen, each armed with a club and an extra revolver. As they neared the outskirts of the crowd, Captain Ward stepped

Left. Albert R. Parsons. *Center*. August Spies. *Right*. Adolph Fischer. *Below left*. George Engel. *(Anarchy and Anarchists.)*

Right. On November 12, 1887, Parsons, Spies, Fischer, and Engel were hanged after a bitter trial and despite pleas for clemency from all over the world. Before the trap was sprung, each man was permitted a final statement. Those of Spies and Parsons were remembered for decades, the first crying, "There will be a time when our silence will be more powerful than the voices you strangle today!" and Parsons calling out, "Let the voice of the people be heard!" And the next day's headlines shrieked: "JUSTICE IS DONE!" and "THE LAW ANSWERS ANARCHY!" *(Anarchy and Anarchists.)*

Left. Rudolph Schnaubelt is now generally believed to be the man who actually threw the bomb. At the time of the Haymarket tragedy, he was arrested, questioned briefly, released, then disappeared forever. *Center*. Louis Lingg. He cheated the gallows by swallowing dynamite in his cell. *Right*. Samuel Fielden. Given life, he was later pardoned. *(Anarchy and Anarchists.)*

Left. Oscar W. Neebe. He was pardoned in the midst of a fifteen-year term. *Center*. Michael Schwab. He also was freed while serving a life sentence. *(Anarchy and Anarchist.) Right*. John Peter Altgeld, the governor who invited political oblivion by pardoning Fielden, Neebe, and Schwab in 1893. *(Authors' Collection.)*

149

In 1885, William Le Baron Jenney started an important era of architectural vitality by designing the first modern steel-skeleton skyscraper, the Home Insurance Building at La Salle and Monroe streets. Using such materials of the new industrial age as structural steel and glass, he gave stimulus to trends that were soon being followed all over the nation. *(Chicago Sun-Times Library.)*

forward and ordered the throng to disperse. Just as the speaker, Samuel Fielden, replied, "We are peaceable," a bomb was thrown.

Its blast reverberated through the dark streets and narrow alleys. Policemen fell dead and dying, dozens of bystanders were maimed. The precise number of dead was never determined, but the awful event sparked a roundup of anarchists and even mild laborites; in a hunt directed by Captain Michael Schaak, many hundreds were packed into jails for weeks. Finally, in an atmosphere atingle with fear and hysteria, Parsons, Spies, and six other anarchists were tried for the murder of one of the policemen. All avowed their anarchistic ideals but denied any connection with the bomb. They insisted they were on trial because of their beliefs, for their struggle in behalf of workers and against bosses. In the end, all were found guilty. Seven were sentenced to death by the vitriolic Judge Joseph Gary but ultimately only four actually went to the gallows. Pleas for amnesty came from thousands, ranging from George Bernard Shaw to Potter Palmer, but the verdict was upheld.

The hangings on November 11, 1887, broke the back of the Chicago anarchist movement, despite some flurries in later years led by Emma Goldman. But there was a stirring aftermath. Six years after the hangings, Governor John Peter Altgeld, responding to pleas and petitions, carefully reviewed the entire trial and granted full pardons to three who had been imprisoned. He scored the prejudicial actions of Judge Gary and called the jurors incompetent. Altgeld brought upon himself vituperation and virtual ruination of his political career, but many who continued to maintain that the case had never really been solved respected him for his deep integrity.

The Haymarket tragedy was a blot on the city's name in the last half of the Elegant Eighties. But another event brought Chicago a different sort of lasting fame. Starting in the mid-1880s and extending well into the early part of the next century, the city experienced a surge of great architectural vitality. The new Chicago-style architecture arose from specific needs: the Great Fire itself, the swift expansion, the rising price of build-

A former member of Jenney's office staff, Louis Henri Sullivan became the greatest architect of that era, although his talents and contributions were not fully realized until long after he died, discouraged and poor and unheralded, in 1924. Sullivan was a believer in modernism, in democratic traditions of artistry; his was an ambivalent theory of design. In none of his creations was his genius morè evident than in the Auditorium, which he and Dankmar Adler began in 1887 and finished at the end of 1889. The part of the building that housed the theater, however, was ready in 1888, as seen at the right, to serve as headquarters for the Republican national convention. *(Harper's Weekly.)*

The theater itself was acoustically perfect. Its ornamentation was rich and majestic, with a great series of arches whose borders and relief bans and an inner lacy pattern were carefully stenciled in gold. For years after the official opening, the t h e a t e r served the city well in the fields of music and opera. *(Art Institute of Chicago.)*

Left. From the side of the Auditorium, as in this striking photograph, one could see Sullivan's tower, an individualistic concept designed for offices. Sullivan's partner, Adler, solved the vexing problem of the building's foundation; fearing that the tower might result in uneven settling and eventual cracking of the masonry, Adler loaded pig iron and bricks equal to the weight of the tower on the lower floors, thereby achieving an even settling before the masons finished the building itself. In the mid-1940s the Auditorium building became Roosevelt University. *(John Szarkowski, University of Minnesota Press.)*

Right. On the South Side, very rich Chicagoans built their homes in this period on Prairie Avenue, seen here from the intersection of Twentieth Street in an illustration from a volume of that day, *Half Century's Progress of the City of Chicago. (International Publishing Company.)*

ing materials, the lack of space. Experiment was essential and, by a happy circumstance of history, there were men in Chicago with the imagination and the talents to answer these needs.

Out of these times came the world's first steel-skeleton skyscraper, the Home Insurance Building at La Salle and Monroe streets, the handiwork of William Le Baron Jenney. As a young man he had visited Manila on one of his father's New Bedford whaling ships and had noticed that the natives used trees as columns and lighter cuts of wood for lateral and diagonal braces, floor supports, and partitions, binding them together at intersections with thongs and pegs. These struc-

tures could withstand heavy winds, even earthquakes. Jenney applied this principle to his ten-story skyscraper, using steel girders as a skeleton for the curtains of light masonry that served as outer walls. In this period others sparkled: Daniel C. Burnham and John Wellborn Root and their Rookery; Root and John Holabird and the Tacoma Building; Root and his Masonic Temple, its 20 stories at State and Randolph streets for some years higher than any. But the prime genius of them all was the imaginatively progressive Louis Henri Sullivan, a believer in an authentically American way of building, of design that was simple and departed from the past. After working

One of the grandest mansions on genteel, wealth-laden Prairie Avenue was that of Marshall Field, whose library is shown here. At a cost of $100,000, it was built for the multimillionaire merchant by Richard Morris Hunt, the famous architect who had also designed the luxurious dwellings of such New York millionaires as William H. Vanderbilt and John Jacob Astor. (*Field Archives.*)

for Jenney and studying in Paris, Sullivan joined Dankmar Adler in 1879. Their noblest achievement was the Auditorium Building at Michigan Avenue and Van Buren Street, a 10-story structure with a hotel and theater for 3,500, plus Sullivan's office tower. The boldest architectural conception of its time, the Auditorium was based on the novel idea of a floating foundation and was first proposed by Ferdinand W. Peck, then in his seventies. Peck fought for it, persuaded people to invest in it, and lived to see the theater's opening night on December 9, 1889, which President Harrison attended and at which Governor Joe Fifer, after hearing Adelina Patti sing "Home, Sweet Home," drew cheers from the glittering audience when he intoned, "We have passed in half a century from the war whoop of the savage to the ravishing strains of a Patti."

There was another kind of construction, too: the immense and elaborate homes of the very wealthy, principally on Prairie Avenue, known as "the street of the sifted few," and on lower Michigan Avenue and on Rush Street. But Potter Palmer surpassed his fellow millionaires. On Lake Shore Drive in a patch of frog ponds, well north of the river, he ordered the construction of a literal castle in Gothic style and here, amid treasures of art and furnishings, expensive vases, silk portières, beneath heavy chandeliers and colored glass windows, Palmer's wife, the former Bertha Honore, ruled Chicago society then and for two decades more. Some wealthy folk sneered at Palmer's seeming foolhardiness in settling so far north, but soon they and others clustered near him and property values, as Palmer had shrewdly anticipated, soared.

Most of these grand homes have long since been razed to make way for sleekly towering apartment houses. But the life, fame, and influence of a vastly different building of that period still persist. In September, two clear-eyed and determined do-gooders, Jane Addams and Ellen Gates Starr, moved into a large old dwelling on South Halsted Street. They named it Hull House, after its owner, and set out to alleviate the poverty and barbaric social conditions of the area, one of the worst in the city. They conducted movements for political reforms and they taught immigrants how to bathe babies; they fought for better living conditions, and they set up a Penny Provident Fund Savings Bank. Miss Addams was a woman possessed with a desire to complete the mobilization of the human spirit and Hull House, as vital a Chicago landmark as any to which boosters of later years pointed pridefully, still stands as a tangible expression of her ideals.

Potter Palmer's Castle, as it appeared in 1889. Palmer was scoffed at by other businessmen in the Elegant Eighties for venturing too far out; his castellated building was a mile north of the river on Lake Shore Drive. But Palmer was to have the final laugh. Property values went up in the area 150 per cent within months after his Gothic palace was finished. (*Chicago Sun-Times Library.*)

Mrs. Potter Palmer ruled society in the 1880s and 1890s, but took an active interest in movements to help working girls and get votes for women. *(Chicago Sun-Times Library.)*

The home of Henry J. Willing, one of Marshall Field's junior partners, was at Rush and Ontario streets, its hallway symbolic of its curlicued splendor. This district was almost on a social par with Prairie Avenue, its French-styled mansions standing gaudily and grandly on the quiet streets. None, however, could compare either in stature or complexity with Palmer's Castle and its battlemented turrets and towers, brown sandstone walls trimmed with gray granite, and a stone balcony. *(Field Archives.)*

Samuel J. Nickerson, one of the founders of the First National Bank, built his luxurious house at Wabash Avenue and Erie Street, whose library and gallery are shown here. A showplace of the 1880s, it was known as "Nickerson's Marble Palace." Many varieties of rare woods decorated the interior, the woodwork was hand-carved throughout, the main hall was of marble, with onyx panels on the walls. In 1958, the building, with its decorative fineries intact, was the headquarters of the American College of Surgeons. *(Chicago Sun-Times Library.)*

Still standing on South Halsted Street is Hull House, which Jane Addams—shown at left in the year of its organization, 1889—made into a world-famed social-service center. (*Chicago Sun-Times Library.*)

Among the myriad activities instituted for the immigrant families in the crowded district around Hull House were classes in various crafts and industries. This group of boy cobblers was photographed for a pictorial series in the 1890s called *Life at Hull House.* (*Chicago Tribune Library.*)

"That Windy City"

IX

As the last decade of the century began, federal census takers swarmed over the city's expanse. And their reports indicated vividly that though Chicago was still young, as the great cities of the world were reckoned, its rise had been astounding.

Its populace of 1,208,676 placed it second only to New York as a major city of the nation. In that year, a record number of buildings were constructed, $48,000,000 worth. Areas where such new structures rose or where verdant parks multiplied scores of Chicagoans could recall as swampland. Where wagon trains had plowed their way over rutted roads into a younger town, railroads by the many dozens now sent their hissing locomotives into ornate depots. Not too long ago all of the city's trade had come to much less than $1,000,000 a year; now, such a mogul as Armour or Swift turned over that amount in only a week. The original Illinois and Michigan Canal having proved inadequate to handle the drainage problems of the billowing city, a Chicago sanitary district had been set up and plans were being completed for a new canal, a complex engineering feat that, before the decade was out, would forever reverse the flow of the river and insure safer water. Rudyard Kipling spoke of the city— so noisy and industrious and wicked and brash— with a shudder: "Having seen it I urgently desire never to see it again. It is inhabited by savages." But John Clark Ridpath, the author of many-volumed works on American and world history, ascended to Sullivan's tower in the Auditorium, looked down upon the city, and decreed: "It is

the marvel not only of our own age and century but of the modern world. Even from the dome of St. Peter's the landscape is by no means so fine, so extended, so full of progress and enthusiasm."

There even was evident, in this materialistic-minded community, a surge for "better things." Committees were organized to demand that the lake front be cleared of all ugly buildings. This campaign was spurred by A. Montgomery Ward, the mail-order-house millionaire whose watchword was "The Lake Front for the people!" and whose nickname—"Watchdog of the Lake Front" —aptly characterized his fight, successful in the long run, to keep the city's front yard free of everything but the Art Institute of Chicago; this building, to be erected three years hence on the site of the decaying Interstate Industrial Exposition Hall, now housed its small and quite undistinguished collection of plaster casts of ancient Egyptian, Greek, and Roman sculpture and a few consequential paintings in a gray-stone Romanesque structure at Michigan Avenue and Van Buren Street. Society folk and music lovers formed the Orchestral Association in 1890, a group that did much to create the Chicago Symphony Orchestra with Theodore Thomas as its leader; Thomas, who would reign over a glowing age of symphonic music in the city for fourteen seasons more, had been a regular visitor with his own group since 1869 and he considered Chicago "the only city on the continent, next to New York, where there is sufficient musical culture to enable me to give a series of fifty successive concerts." A bit more jaundiced in his estimates of Chicago's musical

Below. At the far end of La Salle Street stood the Board of Trade Building. Here were the rooms where fortunes were made and lost, the scenes of frenzy and shouting and clamor that gave Frank Norris inspiration for his famous realistic novel, *The Pit*. The building, erected in 1885, typified the Board of Trade's importance in Chicago's economy, seemingly watching over the city's equivalent of Wall Street, even then lined with financial houses, banks, and corporation offices. It was demolished late in the 1920s and a new structure, the tallest for its time, was erected. The building on the left was The Rookery, another product of the architectural renaissance of the 1880s; in it leading lawyers maintained offices. *(J. W. Taylor.)*

Above. By 1890, the corner of State and Madison streets was already described as "the world's busiest corner." In this photograph of the intersection, the view is west along Madison Street. Within five years the baroque-like Dore block on the northwest corner would be torn down to make way for the Boston Store. *(Chicago Sun-Times Library.)*

From Jackson Boulevard looking south on Michigan Avenue: A view of the Leland Hotel, on the corner, followed by the hoity-toity Richelieu—where everything on the menu was à la carte—and such others as the Masury Building, the Hotel Victoria (the city had at least five similarly named), the old Art Institute, soon to be occupied by the Chicago Club, and the Studebaker Building, which later became the Fine Arts Building. Across from these, on the left, is part of the city's well-protected "front yard." *(Chicago Tribune Library.)*

tastes was the *Inter-Ocean's* music critic, Frederick Grant Gleason, who complained that those who attended performances by touring opera companies came "a little to hear the music, a trifle more to hear the artists . . . but mostly because it is the thing to do."

The capstone of a growing number of educational improvements in this decade was the official incorporation at its start of a new University of Chicago. The old university had gone bankrupt in 1886; the new one was made possible through the largess of John D. Rockefeller, persuaded to make huge grants by Frederick T. Gates, who became the oil magnate's confidential adviser; by Thomas W. Goodspeed, secretary of the Rockefeller-financed Baptist Theological Seminary in Morgan Park; and by William Rainey Harper, brilliant professor of Greek and Hebrew at Yale. Gates and Harper were especially active in snaring the funds for a school of higher learning; as early as 1888 Gates, in a speech to the city's

Baptist ministers, had lamented the poor facilities for higher education. Rockefeller thought a mere college might be adequate; Harper pressed for a full-scale university. Rockefeller gave $600,000. Another $500,000 came from prominent Baptists and businessmen. After some niggling, Marshall Field came up with a donation of land and $300,-000 in cash. While the university's first building, Cobb Lecture Hall, was being constructed on the South Side, Harper scurried around the country recruiting scholars and savants with the dual promise of higher salaries and freedom to engage in original research; on his first faculty he had no fewer than nine ex-college presidents. He secured more and more money, sometimes with difficulty, always through his persuasive ways. On October 1, 1892, the university, destined to become one of the world's most distinguished, opened its doors and the Cobb Hall students walked along singing, "John D. Rockefeller, wonderful man is he, Gives all his spare change to the U. of C.!" By 1902,

159

The first University of Chicago stood at Cottage Grove Avenue at Thirty-fourth Street, on a section of land that once belonged to Stephen A. Douglas. Douglas first offered the land to Presbyterians, who refused it, and in 1854 it was accepted by the Baptists, who built the school. Its first president was the Rev. J. C. Burroughs who left the pastorate of the First Baptist Church. But the institution failed to thrive, debts mounted, and mortgages grew burdensome, and by the middle 1880s the property was sold and the school closed down. The present University of Chicago was begun in 1890. *(Kaufmann-Fabry.)*

this "spare change" would amount to $10,600,-000 and Rockefeller, pleased with what Harper had done, would comment, "I am profoundly thankful that I had anything to do with this affair. The good Lord gave me my money, and how could I withhold it from Chicago?"

Eighteen-ninety was that significant year when there began the literary movement that came to be called the Chicago Renaissance; it ran well into the 1920s almost without flagging and ultimately prompted H. L. Mencken to characterize the city as "the literary capital of the United States." Its writers had a passion for civic self-appraisal and self-criticism, whether they were primarily journalists such as Eugene Field with his sprightly, often sardonic columns in the *News,* or Finley Peter Dunne with his shrewdly observant Mr. Dooley in the *Times-Herald,* or realistic novelists —Hamlin Garland, Henry Blake Fuller, Robert Herrick, or Frank Norris—who were breaking with the established traditions of literary genteel-

ism. Where such visitors as Ridpath had nothing but hyperbolic praise for the city's materialistic gains, most of these men had less roseate reactions; they were caustic about the excesses and pretentions of the wealthy, they made ironic comment on thieving politicians and the presumably respectable businessmen who abetted them, they deplored the fervor of the go-getters and the lack of public taste. Theodore Dreiser, then a young and not very competent reporter plodding the West Side streets for news and absorbing details for the massive novels he was to write, would recall the Chicago of that day as "a very bard of a city, this, singing of high deeds and high hopes, its heavy brogans buried deep in the mire of circumstance." As might be anticipated, eastern critics scoffed at Chicago's "getting up a school of literature overnight," as the *Daily Tribune* put it, "and trying to establish a 'literary school' out of crudity and the froth and fury of the last new things." Yet Sir Walter Besant, in a few short years, would be

The man who brought Chicago its first symphony concerts was this German-born musician, Theodore Thomas. A fine violinist, he came here with his own orchestra in 1862, returned annually—during the labor riots of 1877 he played a five weeks' season with militia stationed around the hall —and in 1891 became conductor of the new Chicago Symphony and remained so until his death in 1905. *(Chicago Sun-Times Library.)*

A year after the Civil War a movement began to open an art school. Such a school was started, but the Great Fire destroyed all its equipment. Undaunted, survivors met regularly for classes until 1882 when Charles L. Hutchinson, a banker and art patron, got other businessmen to back an Art Institute, and commissioned John Root to build this granitic structure, its home until 1892. *(Art Institute of Chicago.)*

In the active journalistic and literary activity of the 1889–90 period, a central gathering point was the Whitechapel Club, whose furnishings included skulls and two full-sized skeletons. Among its better-known members were Finley Peter Dunne (at extreme left), Wallace Rice, editor and poet (fifth from left), and next to him Brand Whitlock, then a young reporter, later a distinguished diplomat. Also members of this aggregation were Eugene Field, George Ade, and John T. McCutcheon, respectively poet-columnist, fictioneer, and editorial cartoonist. *(Chicago Tribune Library.)*

telling fellow-Britons: "There exists in this city of a million inhabitants, which sixty years ago was but a kind of barbican, or advanced post against the red Indian, a company of novelists, poets, and essayists who are united, if not by associations and clubs, at least by an earnest resolution to cultivate letters." And the *Dial,* best of Chicago's literary magazines, avowed happily that all the manifestations, from the new University of Chicago to the rising book-publishing industry, indicated beyond doubt that the city was passing "to a higher and maturer stage of civic existence."

The high point in the diversified decade before the new century came when Chicago, outbidding and outarguing New York, Washington, and St. Louis, staged a multimillion-dollar extravaganza commemorating the four-hundredth anniversary of Columbus' discovery of America. The bidding had started in 1889 when Congress authorized such an exposition and set hearings for a site. Rivalry was tense, insults were flung east and

west; Charles A. Dana, in his *New York Sun,* gave the braggart from the Midwest one of its most adhesive nicknames during the controversy by snickering editorially, "Don't pay any attention to the nonsensical claims of that windy city. Its people couldn't build a world's fair even if they won it."

Ward McAllister, arbiter of New York's society, considered it strange that any exposition should honor Columbus—"In a social way Columbus was an ordinary man"—but hardly anyone in Chicago was likely to agree. This was another opportunity for the city to flaunt its showiness and its virility. A committee of 6,000, certainly the largest in the history of committees anywhere, went to work on all aspects of the forthcoming fair, to be called the World's Columbian Exposition and scheduled, despite inevitable carping from the envious East and despite an impending financial panic, to open in 1893. Daniel H. Burnham, one of the city's best-known architects, was put in charge of construction and about him he gathered some of the country's finest artisans—architects, sculptors, landscape experts, painters.

The actual observance of America's discovery passed and still there was no show. "Don't worry," Burnham assured the citizenry, "we'll make it." And on May 1, 1893, the White City was finished and ready. After two years of haggling and planning and designing and replanning and redesigning, a vast collection of stunning buildings was ready. They housed thousands of exhibits, and were surrounded by gleaming lagoons, a network of highways and thoroughfares, a Midway for

Left. Undoubted leader of religious revival movements in the city was Dwight L. Moody, the heavily bearded man pictured as he appeared in the late 1870s with his musical director, Ira D. Sankey. In their first popular campaigns in Great Britain, they introduced their famed hymnbooks. In his Chicago years, Moody was one of the men most deeply involved in the organization of the Young Men's Christian Association. He founded Sunday schools, missions, and the large Christian training school and church which bears his name and is considered the "West Point of Christian Service." (*Moody Bible Institute.*)

In 1891, a photographer named Sigmund Krausz took his camera into the Chicago streets and persuaded dozens of persons to pose for him. Later he published the best of the pictures in *Street Types of Chicago*. His hardships, as he told it, were manifold: "I was compelled for weeks and months to haunt the crowded thoroughfares, the fashionable avenues, and the dingy alleys . . . I do not wish to speak of the many ludicrous and unpleasant experiences my self-imposed task has brought upon me; suffice it to say that after enduring frequent insults. escaping a fight with a courageous dude, being taken for a medical student in search of subjects for the dissecting room, and barely avoiding arrest . . . I am happy to present the *Street Types of Chicago* to the favorable notice of the public." These are some of his photographs, with his own captions. (*Street Types of Chicago*.)

"Matches! Flypaper!"

"Scissors!"

"Ah there!"

"Out for a Stroll."

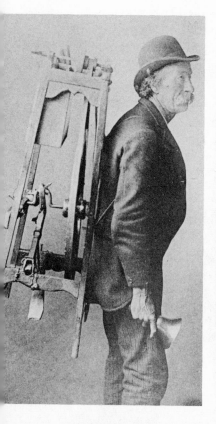

Above. Daniel C. Burnham, the architect who was in charge of construction for the World's Columbian Exposition and later fathered the Burnham Plan for beautifying and improving the city. *(Century Magazine.)*

Below. The men who designed the exposition and its buildings were either already famous or were propelled toward fame as a result of their work in 1893. Some of them are pictured here. With Burnham on the far left they are George B. Post, architect; Montgomery B. Pickett, secretary of works; Henry Van Brunt, architect; Frank D. Millett, director of decoration; Maitland Armstrong, artist; Colonel Edward Rice, commandant; Augustus St. Gaudens, sculptor; Henry Codman, landscape architect; George Maynard, architect; Charles McKim, architect; Ernest Graham, one of Burnham's assistants, later a famous architect; Dion Geraldine, general superintendent. *(Chicago Then and Now.)*

pleasure seekers—spreading over the sandy 550 acres of dismal quagmire in what had been half-completed Jackson Park. And as the visitors came, slowly at first but, with the summer months, in greater and greater numbers, they saw all the wonders gathered from everywhere, wonders electrical and industrial, wonders artistic and aesthetic. Here were such newfangled devices as an intramural train with a third rail electrically stimulated, first of its kind in the world; a huge network of incandescent lighting; a telephone hookup on which one could hear concerts from New York; engines and water wheels and refrigeration machines and fire trucks soon to make horse-drawn engines obsolete; awesome naval guns and hydraulic presses and Edison's Kinetoscope, a camera and phonograph working in perfect unison. There were valued paintings in the Fine Arts Palace and cured meats from the Chicago stockyards; rose plantations and French tapestries and model tenements proving that people could live on $500 a year; a Canadian ten-ton cheese, largest in the world; the great Yerkes telescope, given by the traction king, Charles Tyson Yerkes. And if these and so many more were not enough, there came royal visitors from Spain—the haughty Infanta Eulalia representing its rulers—to gawk and be gawked at.

And there was the Ferris wheel, that engineering novelty imported from Europe. No matter by which road one approached the exposition, it was the first thing to meet the eye. Its 36 cars were

filled day and night with thrill-seekers. "Candor compels the confession," admitted a *Harper's Weekly* reporter, "that one does not step into the cars of the wheel without some trepidation. . . . Nothing like it was ever built or attempted before."

The Ferris wheel remained an everlasting symbol of that show, but an equally historic lure was the lithe young Armenian dancer who gyrated in the Midway's Streets of Cairo. Her real name was Fahreda Mahzar but then and for all time thereafter—until her death in Chicago forty-three years later, a dainty old woman deploring nudity and vulgarity on the stage—she was "Little Egypt."

And then, by the end of October, it was all over. Down came all the buildings except the Arts Palace which, somewhat remodeled and refashioned, ultimately became the Rosenwald Museum of Science and Industry. The flamboyant Midway soon was the University of Chicago's Midway and Jackson Park bloomed to full size. Many thought that the massive exposition had set new standards of civic beauty and had given visitors an idea of what a city could be like. Louis Sullivan was not among them. He lamented the fact that all the architecture—his own Transportation Building, unadorned and sleek, was the exception—had reverted to the past for inspiration. What the throngs

Eager to be his beloved city's World's Fair mayor, the elder Carter Harrison ran again and won. This caricature has him drawing aside the World's Columbian Exposition curtain. *(Chicago Sun-Times Library.)*

A striking view of the exposition looking south from across the west end of the basin. On the left is the Agricultural Building and the Machinery Hall, and on the right is the elaborately wrought McMonnies Fountain. *(C. D. Arnold.)*

Symbolic of the classical motifs was Richard Morton Hunt's Administration Building. Many thought that the big fair helped make art manifest to the American consciousness, but such men as Louis Sullivan vowed that this kind of styling, which predominated the buildings, set back architecture in the United States half a century. Sullivan's own comparatively unadorned Transportation Building was hailed by critics, especially Europeans, as "appropriately modern . . . and cyclonic." *(Century Magazine.)*

really had seen, he wrote later, was "a naked exhibitionism of charlantry in the higher feudal and domineering culture, conjoined with expert salesmanship of the materials of decay." Perhaps this was an extreme view, for out of the event Burnham did develop a system of city planning; but there were many who agreed with Sullivan, and for scores of visitors the memory of the magnificent landscaping, architecture, and educational exhibits was outlived by that of Little Egypt as she danced her hootchy-kootchy to the sound of a mournful flute.

Even as the Boosters and Boomers exulted over the glories of the big fair, the city was beset again by fearful depression. People died of cold and hunger in that winter of 1893–94. Not far from magnificent new mansions the homeless huddled in hallways and the hungry shuffled along in lengthy bread lines. The city hall corridors were kept open, giving shelter to 2,000 each night; squadrons of unemployed formed street-sweeping brigades in exchange for a bowl of soup. Famine raged in the poorer districts, and Jane Addams and her associates worked twenty hours a day seeking help for the destitute. Hundreds of unfortunates wandered southward and hundreds more joined "General" Jacob Coxey's "Commonwealth of Christ" Army as it marched off to seek aid in Washington. The city was bleak and dark-hued.

As in previous depressions, conflict arose. On the southern outskirts of the city, George M. Pullman had put up his model company town, named it for himself; he wanted the people who built his sleeping cars to be near their work and to be happy in that work. When panic struck the nation, Pullman, like other industrialists, slashed wages but neglected to reduce rents or food costs. In May 1894, a committee of his workers called on him to ask for a restoration of the wage cuts. Two days later several of these men were fired, whereupon all of the Pullman employees, most of them members of Eugene Victor Debs' American Railway Union, walked out.

Debs and his officers, meeting in convention that June at Chicago, sought to negotiate an end to the strike. Pullman refused to arbitrate. The strike spread. The A.R.U. instructed its members, 150,-000 throughout the land, to cease handling Pullman cars. Someone devised a plan of hitching federal mail cars to Pullmans so that when the strikers turned off a Pullman they would technically be charged with interfering with the United States mails. A federal judge in Chicago enjoined Debs and his officers from such actions. To enforce the order President Cleveland sent two companies of infantry to Chicago over the protests of

One of the exposition's joys was a visit to the Midway, a stretch of sideshows and replicas of foreign villages. On this plaisance was the Irish v i l l a g e, Old Vienna, a Moorish palace with a "chamber of horrors," an Egyptian temple, South Sea Islanders, the World's Congress of Beauty, Buffalo Bill and his Indians and, most famous of all, "Little Egypt." (*Wide World.*)

Neither beautiful buildings nor even the Ferris wheel could match the ultimate fame of Little Egypt, the dark-eyed minx who danced the undulating hootchy-kootchy in the Midway's Streets of Cairo, a prominent feature of the World's Columbian Exposition built in Chicago in 1893. *(Authors' Collection.)*

Below. Presented for the first time in America, the Ferris wheel was a crowd favorite. Its thirty-six cars revolved leisurely and at the topmost position, rose 265 feet in the air. *(Chicago Sun-Times Library.)*

Governor Altgeld. When, on July 6, the soldiers tried to operate the trains, the strikers ran wild, ripping up tracks and overturning freight cars. Next day Debs was arrested and sent to a suburban jail for six months, and shortly the strike was broken; but the rancor and bitterness engendered in these dark months lasted a long time.

The year that saw the big exposition and the depression also signaled the start of one of the most efficient political affiliations in the city's history, that of the flamboyant, showy John "Bathhouse John" Coughlin, Democratic alderman from the wicked First Ward, and Michael "Hinky Dink" Kenna, a mite of a man with a genius for organization. Coughlin was a former bathhouse attendant, Kenna the owner of the Workingmen's Exchange Saloon on Clark Street; together they built an organization of saloonkeepers, gamblers, pimps, pickpockets, and brothel owners who would help them, term after term, hold their City Council seats

October 9 in that exposition year was Chicago Day, commemorating the Great Fire. More than 700,000 people came on foot, by carriage, sat inside and clung to the outsides of cable cars, gripping their special Chicago Day tickets in their hands (shown below) and swarming happily all over the fairgrounds. They watched pageants depicting incidents in the city's history; a record number of children were lost and found again; police reported they were unable to handle many segments of the crowd; and everyone went home happy. As the great fair drew to a close late in October, the city was shaken by the assassination of Mayor Harrison in the doorway of his Ashland Avenue home by an embittered office seeker. The flags went to half-mast and the people mourned. Many recalled one of Harrison's rhapsodies to the city: "Genius is but audacity, and the audacity of the 'wild and woolly West' and of Chicago has chosen a star, and has looked upward to it, and knows nothing that it cannot accomplish." (*Chicago Sun-Times Library.*)

and a power of political muscularity. In a city where wealth and culture rubbed against corruption and viciousness, in a First Ward where gin mills, miserable cribs, dime hotels, and free-lunch saloons hovered near great office buildings, the Kenna-Coughlin combine thrived. These "Lords of the Levee" helped secure protection from arrest or eviction for the madams of the thriving vice district. They bought votes from bums and drunks for fifty cents apiece, they participated in boodle payments made to crooked aldermen by such barons as Charles Tyson Yerkes, who controlled the traction system and reached out for more and more power. Coughlin composed terrible poetry or, at best, recited bad poems written for him by reporters, wore orange vests and green trousers and lavender tail coats; Kenna spoke not ten words a day, chewed on cigars, and amassed voters and a fortune. Together they staged, annually, for more than a decade, First Ward balls at which

The exposition had opened its gates in the face of impending financial panic. When the depression hit, it hit hard. The streets were filled with the homeless and many begged for food and shelter. In the city hall—as depicted here—hundreds slept nightly in the corridors. The city's winter of 1893–94 was the most horrible in its history, with people dying of starvation, and freezing to death. The times were ripe for strife and violence, and both came in the form of widespread strikes and fighting in the streets. *(Harper's Weekly.)*

the denizens of such vice districts as the Bad Lands, Bed Bug Row, and Hell's Half Acre mingled with political leaders and police captains. Reformers denounced the festivals as saturnalian orgies and Dionysian festivals; Kenna called them lalapaloozas as he and his cohorts counted the receipts.

Among the visitors to Hinky Dink's Saloon in 1893 was William T. Stead, the English editor come to see the city he considered "one of the wonders of the nineteenth century." Stead went elsewhere, too: to the Prairie Avenue mansions, to the brothels, to the City Council chambers to talk with boodling aldermen; to tax records, schools, jails, and churches. Then he loosed his blast, a sensational book of more than 400 pages, *If Christ Came to Chicago,* in which he named names, excoriated Yerkes, called boodling alder-

men "the swine of our civilization," and shouted for reform. Stead's revelations excited some and titillated others, but the serious-minded, led by Lyman J. Gage, formed the Civic Federation and vowed to fight thieving politicians and rascals everywhere.

Stead's sulphurous book disclosed details about sections of the First Ward that constituted as notorious a vice district as existed anywhere in the world. He told of interviews with the premier madam of the time, Carrie Watson—"She has made a fortune out of her trade in the bodies of her poorer sisters." He printed a Black List of owners, renters, tenants, and taxpayers of "property used for immoral purposes." This district then centered near Van Buren Street along Clark Street, Customs House Place, and Plymouth Place. But another similar red-light district was developing farther south in an area bounded by Clark Street, Wabash Avenue, and Twenty-second and Eighteenth streets. Here, in this horrendous Levee, was packed every form of vice: brothels, saloons, wine rooms, and dives in which every kind of depravity was practiced. Its pimps had formed

So important was the labor strife of 1893–94 that Frederick Remington was sent to Chicago to record some of the events. This pictorial report shows a scene in the Union Stockyards with wild-eyed strikers yelling to federal troops, according to Remington, "To hell with the government!" *(Harper's Weekly.)*

When Eugene V. Debs called the members of his American Railway Union out on strike, much of the city's traffic and commerce was paralyzed. W. A. Rogers, the magazine artist, saw Debs as a kind of despot and depicted him sitting astride a highway of trade that has been temporarily turned off its course; "King Debs" was the name affixed to the labor leader by those who disapproved of the strike. *(Harper's Weekly.)*

The daring and inventive photographer of the era was George R. Lawrence, better known as "Flashlight" Lawrence. A typical exploit of his was to make one of the first aerial photographs from a balloon near the Armour Plant, preparations for which, as can be seen above, were complicated and well guarded. *(Chicago Tribune Library.)*

A neighborhood variety store of the 1890s, with price lists for a diversified selection of articles, from the *Chicago Tribune*—then calling itself merely "Chicago's Greatest Daily"—for only one cent to Climax Plug Tobacco, Palm's Bread, or Moorish Sherbet for five cents. *(Chicago Tribune Library.)*

Above. After the World's Columbian Exposition the city elevated lines began stretching rapidly into sections of the city other than the South Side, whose "Alley L" was the first in 1892. This is a photograph of one of the cars on the Lake Street line, complete with locomotive named Clarence A. (*Chicago Sun-Times Library.*)

Right. In the 1890s at an all-night restaurant such as the one at the left a hungry man, for an outlay of only fifteen cents, could buy a meal consisting of steak, pie, and coffee. (*Chicago Tribune Library.*)

Michael Kenna, called "Hinky Dink," at the start of his career as politician and one of the monarchs of the city's lurid First Ward. (*Authors' Collection.*)

Builder and corrupter, Charles Tyson Yerkes bought legislators by the dozens, paid for favorable laws, served as model for Theodore Dreiser's Chicago novel *The Titan*. (*Chicago Tribune Library.*)

John Coughlin, called "Bathhouse John," as a new alderman in 1892. Together he and Kenna ruled the First Ward for nearly half a century. (*Authors' Collection.*)

a Cadets Protective Association. Its occupants included thieves, dope addicts, pickpockets, murderers, sexual degenerates. And its showplace, starting in 1900, was the internationally famous and infamous Everleigh Club, at 2131-33 Dearborn Street. Two Kentucky sisters, Ada and Minna Everleigh, operated this elegant establishment that, in its riotous heyday, became the best-known bordello in the whole world. Each of two entrances led into perfume-sprayed hallways where the visitor able to afford it was met by a diamond-bedecked Minna and conducted either into the music room, library, or art gallery, there to meet a fully-clad, dignified whore; there was no vulgar parading as in the lesser brothels. Each girl's room was furnished as she wished it to be, most of them with reds and golds; each room had a gold spittoon and a device that shot perfume into the air. Prices ranged from $10.00 to $50.00, depending on the type of service the girl of one's choice was required to render. The chef was the best in the nation; the champagnes were of the choicest vintage. The Everleighs, well protected by political payoffs, prospered year after year; ultimately they amassed a million dollars in cash, art treasures, and $25,000 in customers' I O Us. Reformers constantly harangued Carter Henry Harrison the Younger almost weekly after his election as mayor in 1897, demanding that he do something about the Levee. He gave periodic cleanup orders to his various police chiefs, but nothing of real consequence happened to the Everleighs and the Levee until the sisters issued, in the summer of 1911, a booklet with photographs of its various parlors and rooms. This kind of advertising so incensed Harrison that he insisted the place be closed. Frantic efforts —by Coughlin and Kenna, among others—were made to countermand the order, but Harrison remained obdurate. The Everleigh sisters departed to live out their old age in New York with their fortune and their gold piano, but the Levee continued its evil ways, with frequent interruptions by anti-vice forces, for at least three more years.

Less colorful than his father, Harrison was just as popular; he won three two-year terms and

Gathering place in the First Ward for politicians, gamblers, and gawkers was Kenna's Workingmen's Exchange. At the bar, in the dapper white trousers, is Hinky Dink himself entertaining visitors including, at Kenna's right, Thomas McNally, called "First Search" McNally because, as a deputy coroner, he always managed to go through the pockets of corpses ahead of anyone else. *(Authors' Collection.)*

Most riotous of Chicago's revels for nearly a decade were the First Ward balls staged by Coughlin and Kenna to raise campaign funds. To them came Levee madams and their favorite girls, panders, thieves, gamblers, burglars, politicians, and society folk. Ultimately, reformers, after persistently hammering away at the excesses and goings on—some of which John T. McCutcheon caught impressionistically in this *Collier's* magazine sketch—compelled the lords of the Levee to give them up. *(John T. McCutcheon Collection.)*

No more renowned ladies of the Levee existed anywhere than Ada and Minna Everleigh, who enriched themselves by maintaining the best-known bordello in the whole world in the Levee's palmiest days early in the present century. In this rare photograph the sisters are at either end of a tallyho, b o u n d, with some of their most attractive girls, for a day at the Washington Park races. *(Walter Scholl Collection.)*

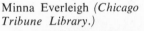

Minna Everleigh *(Chicago Tribune Library.)*

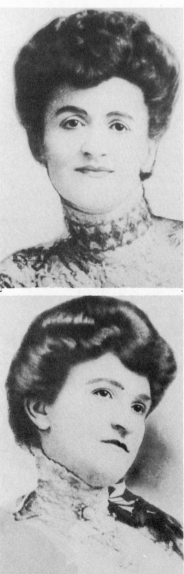

Ada Everleigh *(Chicago Tribune Library.)*

became the city's first four-year mayor, from 1911 to 1915. Besides his anti-Levee assault, he battled vigorously against Yerkes and the Gray Wolves of the City Council. Interestingly, in his ultimate defeat of Yerkes' attempts to buy beneficial legislation, Harrison was aided by those First Ward potentates, Bathhouse John Coughlin and Hinky Dink Kenna.

An amazing controversy during much of Harrison's tenure centered around the efforts of a mustachioed eccentric, George Wellington Streeter, and his rangy wife, Maria, to retain squatters' rights to immeasurably valuable property on the lake shore. This battle had its origins back in July 1886, when Cap Streeter had beached his excursion boat in a squall on a sand bar in Lake Michigan a block south of Chicago Avenue. Instead of freeing the vessel, Streeter built a makeshift breakwater and settled down there. In time more sand settled around the boat, ultimately covering the distance from ship to shore. Streeter campaigned to have other squatters join him in his little kingdom; he sold lots, gave out interviews, guzzled whisky, kept a rifle by his side. N. Kellogg Fairbank, one of the millionaires who found the sight of Streeter's shanty distasteful whenever he stared out across the sandy wastes from his own mansion, sought to oust him. But Streeter would not budge. Constables were sent. Later there were exchanges

Toward the south end of Chicago's Levee from 1900 to 1910, the Everleigh Club, consisting of the two houses on the extreme right, were the most affluent, the most expensive, and the best known. Extending down Dearborn Street from Nos. 2131–33 were such other establishments as Ed Weiss' Saratoga Club, Georgie Spencer's, French Emma Duval's, Maurice Van Bever's Sans Souci. *(Walter Scholl Collection.)*

This fantastically bedecked room was once described by a visitor to the Everleigh Club as "a whore's dream of what a Japanese throne room must be like." And that is precisely what the room was called. It was reproduced in an advertising booklet issued by the sisters touting the entire establishment as "a most sumptuous place . . . long famed for its luxurious furnishings, famous paintings, and statuary, and its elaborate and artistic decorations." *(Everleigh Club Booklet.)*

Alcove of a typical Everleigh Club love chamber. "One never feels the winter's chill or summer's heat in this luxurious resort," stated the booklet. "Fortunate, indeed, with all the comforts of life surrounding them, are the members of the Everleigh Club." *(Everleigh Club Booklet.)*

Another Levee notable for generations was Vic Shaw, whose real name was Emma Ludwig. Long after the Everleighs and their associates had departed, Madam Vic was still active in her trade at the age of seventy, operating in a decrepit mansion that once had been the home of the Armour family. (*Walter Scholl Collection.*)

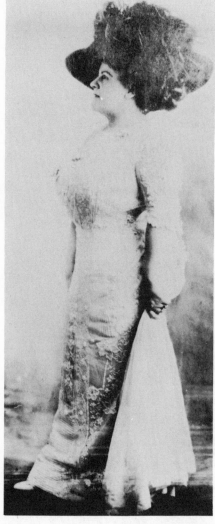

Familiar sights on Levee streets were bands of well-meaning visitors come to pray for the souls of the residents, as these are doing outside the Sans Souci resort. One of the largest revival meeting processions into what its leader, Gipsy Smith, called a "Hellhole of Sin," came late in 1909. The Levee residents and their owners cackled and jeered, but their heyday as an organized community of vice was about to end. (*Walter Scholl Collection.*)

The man who began destruction of the Levee in 1910 was Carter Henry Harrison the Younger. He acted after a copy of the *Everleigh Club Booklet* fell into his hands. Harrison was mayor then, as well liked as his father had been. This photograph, taken by Harry Bryan Owsley, was one of Harrison's favorites, perhaps because it enabled him to use a prize campaign quip: "Chicago is fortunate in having a mayor who keeps his hands in his own pockets." *(Chicago Tribune Library.)*

One of the doughtiest battlers against crime and crooked politics was George E. Cole, pudgy and pugnacious stationer. As head of the Municipal Voters' League he managed to defeat aldermanic boodlers and insure clean elections, labeled the mightiest traction magnet of the time "Yerkes the Boodler" and for a while aroused a great part of Chicago to seek governmental reforms. *(Authors' Collection.)*

If you were in society in the 1900s, you had to attend the races regularly, and you went in your own carriage or, as this group, in a tallyho. The prominent Chicagoans and guests here are (left to right) Mrs. Della Caton, who later became the second wife of Marshall Field; Franklin MacVeagh, the wealthiest of the wholesale grocers; Mrs. Arthur Meeker, a South Side social leader; Miss Irene Catlin, a guest from St. Louis; Mrs. Fred Ames, Miss Marjorie Burns, and Arthur Meeker. *(Chicago Historical Society.)*

Shortly before his death in 1899, one of Chicago's best-known citizens, Joseph Medill, posed for this photograph with his grandchildren. The old gentleman is flanked by (seated) Robert R. McCormick, later editor and publisher of the *Tribune,* and Joseph Medill Patterson, who wrote Socialist novels, joined McCormick at the *Tribune,* ultimately founded the *New York Daily News,* and Eleanor Patterson, who became a countess and newspaper publisher, and Medill McCormick, who represented Illinois in the United States Senate. Medill's deathbed farewell is reported to have been: "What is the news?" *(Chicago Tribune Library.)*

180

In the 1890s Chicago had the world's largest mail-order houses in Montgomery, Ward and Company, which had originated in 1872, and in Sears, Roebuck and Company, organized later but with a rising executive named Julius Rosenwald as vice-president, already a rival for all that an American farmer and small-town dweller might need, from baby carriages to shrouds.

A. Montgomery Ward. (*Montgomery, Ward and Company.*)

Richard W. Sears. (*Sears, Roebuck and Company.*)

Alva W. Roebuck. (*Sears, Roebuck and Company.*)

Ever since the invention of the telephone, Chicago was an extensive user of the valuable device and from the earliest days of its service was one of the country's major long-distance switching centers.

These are the liquid-voiced Hello Girls in the switching room of the Main Exchange Building in 1902. (*Illinois Bell Telephone Company.*)

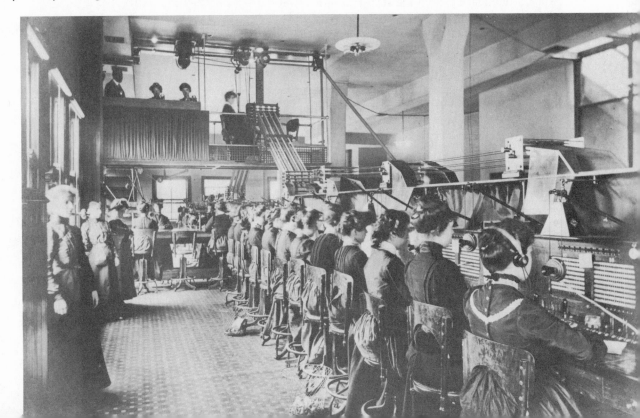

of shots. Suits were filed. And still Streeter stayed in his tawdry domain, now grown to 180 acres. His lawyers maintained that the site on which Streeter now lived was outside the city limits, that he had legal possession. For years the conflict continued. Streeter gathered adherents, proclaimed his territory the District of Lake Michigan, subject neither to laws of Chicago nor Illinois.

His downfall began after a man was shot in one of the battles in Streeterville. He served nine months in the state penitentiary, emerged to renew the struggle, took to himself a new Ma Streeter, half his age but just as fierce. There were more writs, more arrests, and finally, in 1918, deputies followed out a court order to destroy Streeter's home and remove him. He left, vowing to come back. But two years later he was dead of pneumonia, his Streeterville an area even then under consideration as an eventual site for university buildings, apartment houses, and great skyscrapers.

If Streeter and his didoes constituted one of the era's ludicrous events, surely the most tragic occurrence was on the afternoon of December 30, 1903. In the "absolutely fireproof" Iroquois Theater a happy audience sat applauding the performers in *Mr. Bluebeard*. Unknown to the audience, a strip of gauze on the proscenium arch drapery ignited from a sputtering, open arc light; then a tiny flame ran up the strip and lit a velvet drape. Soon flimsy scenery was afire. Men, women, and children rose in panic. The play's star, Eddie Foy, stepped forward in his grotesque costume, calling, "Please be quiet! There is no danger!" The orchestra, at his nod, struck up a tune. Some calm was restored. But then a length of blazing muslin drifted down to the stage; more fiery fragments fell. In an instant the auditorium was a place of horror, with maddened, shrieking, struggling people heading for exits, some of which were locked. The asbestos curtain jammed halfway down. Flames billowed out over the orchestra pit, roared upward into the dome, and licked the balconies. When it was over—it all happened in fifteen awful minutes—596 were dead and all of Chicago, it seemed, had a loved one to mourn.

A happier aspect of show business was the de-

The indomitable eccentrics, Ma and Cap Streeter. *(Chicago Historical Society.)*

velopment of Chicago as the nation's foremost movie-producing center. In 1905 George K. Spoor joined with Gilbert M. Anderson, better known as "Bronco Billy," to form the Essanay Film Company, working first out of a studio on Wells Street near North Avenue, later in 1908 building on Argyle Street on the North Side what was then the biggest movie studio in the country. There, Spoor turned out several two- and three-reelers a week, on a budget of $1,000 for a picture that often yielded $20,000 in rentals. Locations for Spoor's "epics" were usually the banks of the new Sanitary District Canal just north of Foster Avenue. Essanay stars included Lillian Drew and Beverly Bayne and Francis X. Bushman, first of the movie idols, and Ben Turpin, who had started as a studio handyman, and Wallace Beery and Gloria Swanson, who were wed while working for Spoor. Ring Lardner wrote scripts, William Gillette appeared in Essanay's version of *Sherlock Holmes*. By 1917, however, suits were filed seeking to break up a producers' trust of which Essanay was an important part; the Supreme Court ordered the trust smashed, Spoor's firm collapsed, and the moviemaking industry vanished from Chicago.

Eddie Foy, great comedian and valiant hero. *(Samuel Stratton Collection.)*

Fire's aftermath: the devastated auditorium of the Iroquois Theater after the tragedy of the afternoon of December 30, 1903. Flames spread with terrifying speed during a performance of *Mr. Bluebeard* and in a span from 3:15 to 3:30 P.M. 596 persons lost their lives. *(Samuel Stratton Collection.)*

Above. Then, as today, Chicago took enormous pride in its lake-front beaches. Pavilions were built out into Lake Michigan, as here in Jackson Park, and on oppressively hot days the best way to cool off was to frolic and splash in the lake, where the temperatures always were 10 to 15 degrees lower than they were as little as two miles inland. *(Kaufmann-Fabry.)*

Right. If you were more athletically minded, you got yourself, in this era, a high-wheeler and went out to Lincoln Park and rode on its new pathways. But first you posed for a photograph near the flower displays. *(Kaufmann-Fabry.)*

Always a good baseball town, Chicago was especially proud of Charles Comiskey's White Sox in 1906. The team, despite its reputation as the Hitless Wonders, won nineteen straight victories that season, and then went on to whip the powerful Chicago Cubs in baseball's first intracity World Series. In derbied mufti, "The Old Roman" is flanked by his son, Louis, and an associate, Charles Fredericks. (*John C. Hoffman Collection.*)

A popular spectator sport was watching balloon races in White City, a South Side amusement park named and superficially modeled after the World's Fair original of 1893. (*Fred Tuckerman.*)

Chicago's movie industry was once the biggest of its kind anywhere. On this Essanay lot in 1907 George K. Spoor's cameramen are filming a movie with a religious theme. Beyond the rear fence are the outskirts of a cemetery from whose graves wreaths and bouquets were borrowed by the moviemakers for scene settings. *(E. B. Cregier.)*

Plans, Wars and Politics

X

Ever since the end of the World's Columbian Exposition, Daniel Burnham had been obsessed with the need for planning, for refashioning, and revitalizing the growing city. What had been done on the sandy tracts on the South Side could be done again, larger and better, in a multiplicity of ways, for the entire lake front, for the commercial district, for the slums—Jacob Riis said they were the worst he had ever seen, comparable to the squalid sections of European cities—and for riverbanks, the parks, even the suburbs.

As early as 1896 Burnham had shown, to any organization that would look, his sketches for a beautified lake front, with a drive along the south shore, a lagoon, islands, beaches, and parks. People listened, talked, approved or disapproved, debated, formed committees. Meanwhile, Burnham went off to work in Washington, to head a commission to study the redevelopment of the capital; the plan he submitted in 1902 marks the real birth of city planning in America. He did similar jobs for Cleveland, San Francisco, and Manila. Then Chicago was ready for him. The city's Commercial Club, in 1905, asked Burnham to draw up an extensive and detailed plan. For three years Burnham and his assistant, Edward H. Bennett, and their draftsmen and engineers and artists worked in offices on the seventeenth floor of the Railway Exchange Building at Michigan Avenue and Jackson Boulevard, from which height they could see the expanse of land, water, and sky.

And in 1908 Burnham was ready with his charts, maps, and drawings and his famous pro-

nunciamento: "Make no little plans; they have no magic to stir men's blood, and probably themselves will not be realized. Make big plans; aim high in hope and work, remembering that a noble, logical diagram once recorded will never die, but long after we are gone will be a living thing, asserting itself with ever-growing insistency. Remember that our sons and grandsons are going to do things that would stagger us. Let your watchword be order and your beacon beauty."

Having thus spoken, Burnham unfolded his plan. Picturizations of the future had been drawn by Jules Guerin, a well-known artist. The words and the ideas were those of Burnham. He saw, for instance, a downtown Chicago of the future in the style of central Paris, with buildings no higher than eight stories and all uniform. He envisaged a comprehensive park system; a thoroughfare extending on Congress Street as a principal gateway to the West; riverbanks beautified with parks and restaurants; a vast civic center in the downtown area; a widened Michigan Avenue with a two-level bridge at the river; development of the lake front from Jackson Park to Wilmette with lagoons, yacht harbors, and islands in the water and a boulevard system on land reclaimed from the lake; a smooth drive connecting the north and south sections; a system of radial highways inside and outside the city linked by bow-shaped boulevards; a transportation system sufficient to fill all the city's needs.

This new Chicago Plan had to be sold, and such men as Charles H. Wacker and Walter D. Moody and Frank I. Bennett went about selling

A sight to remember—with a shudder. A traffic tieup of monumental proportions was this one around 1910 at the corners of Washington and Dearborn streets. *(Chicago Tribune Library.)*

State and Madison streets, early in 1913. Looking north on "the great street" from Madison, one sees the new Mandel Brothers store, and the large building down the street, its world-famous corner clocks jutting out over the passing crowds, is Marshall Field and Company. *(Kaufmann-Fabry.)*

In the Burnham Plan to revamp Chicago, this was an artist's conception of how the city could be developed in the area from Twenty-second Street to Chicago Avenue looking eastward from a proposed civic center to Grant Park and Lake Michigan. Chicago still is debating the merits of a civic center and other as yet unrealized aspects of Burnham's proposals. *(Chicago Plan Commission.)*

One of the city's biggest processions was on Preparedness Day, June 3, 1916. In the several years immediately preceding the country's entry into World War II there were flurries of controversy about excessive pro-German sentiments in the community and the city's mayor, William Hale Thompson, was labeled "Kaiser Bill" because he expressed anti-Allied sentiments and was cool toward greeting representatives of the British and French forces. *(Chicago Tribune Library.)*

it. Opposition developed; when the backers of the plan sought an ordinance widening Twelfth Street they were denounced by property owners for their "rich man's scheme." When they proposed the extension of Michigan Avenue north of the river they were charged with seeking a "boulevard for wealthy motorists." But they and others persisted and, in time, a number of the Burnham ideas won out.

Already some of the Burnham proposals had been anticipated in another form; in crowded tenement areas, for instance, new playgrounds had been built by the dozens, although this was far less the result of any Commercial Club ideas than those of the sainted Jane Addams. She and other social workers had been instrumental, too, in expressing sentiments that led, after considerable wrangling, to the establishment of the first Juvenile Court in the country, a model for other cities. Beyond the public and critical opposition to the Burnham Plan—Lewis Mumford once referred to its detail as so much "municipal cosmetic"—another obvious barrier to the expenditures essential to fulfillment of its worth-while aspects was the advent of World War I. Although the city was almost as pro-German as it was pro-Ally in the early stages of the fighting in Europe, once the country was in the war public response was enthusiastic. "Slow to wrath," intoned a *Herald* editorialist, "America in a day becomes strong and terrible." As might be anticipated, industry bustled: extra shifts at the packing houses; shell-machining equipment at the Pullman plant; garment factories working overtime turning out nearly $300,000,000 worth of clothing for the armed forces; machine-gun casts and ammunition wagons emerging from reaper factories.

An ugly aftermath of the war developed in the year after the war's end. Large numbers of Negroes had come up from the South to work in factories. Fights often broke out between whites and Negroes seeking homes in restricted areas. On a steaming day in July 1919, an incident on a South Side beach touched off five days of rioting and carnage in which 22 Negroes and 16 whites lost their lives and some 500 persons

The tragedy of the *Eastland*. On July 24, 1915, pic-
nickers boarded this remodeled excursion boat and
prepared to go on a Western Electric outing. For no
apparent reason the boat suddenly listed in the Chicago River at the Clark Street Bridge and turned
quickly on its side. Of the 2,000 persons aboard, 812
were drowned. *(Chicago Sun-Times Library.)*

were injured. Studies were made, dozens of them, but little was done to alleviate basic conditions that lay beneath the violent outbreaks.

With the end of World War I, too, came prohibition—and the outbreak of new and fiercer hostilities within the city itself and its suburbs as gangsters and brigands wrangled and killed to gain immense powers and illicit profits.

Since 1915 the ruler of the scattered remnants of the Levee had been Big Jim Colosimo, a swart braggart, a profligate spender, and a vice lord since his youth. His chief aide was Johnny Torrio, a New Yorker with a soft voice, the brain of a master organizer, and a quietly ruthless way about him. When Harrison smashed the Levee, Colosimo had sent Torrio to surrounding hamlets to establish whole communities of brothels and gambling joints. With a lavish hand, Torrio corrupted village officials and built a mighty empire for his bulbous boss and, as it soon developed, for himself.

Prohibition added greatly to Big Jim's wealth. He controlled the Italian community that had gone into the business of cooking alcohol and his gangsters, under Torrio's direction, were shouldering their way into control of the wholesale-liquor racket. But Big Jim's new affluence was not to last long. On May 11, 1920, he went to his café to keep an appointment. He waited past the set time, then prepared to leave. In the lobby, two shots came from behind a pillar and Colosimo fell dead. Johnny Torrio, interviewed by police, wept bitterly. "Me kill Jim? Why, Jim and me were like brothers." Questioned briefly and also released was a greasy, scar-faced young hoodlum, an Alphonse Caponi, recently imported by Torrio from the Five Points section of Brooklyn.

The mourning over, Torrio tightened his organization. He forced himself into partnership with the owners of several pre-prohibition breweries and allotted to the bandits, thieves, burglars, and kidnapers in his syndicate the districts in which they were to handle beer and liquor shipments, deliveries, and collections. None was to stray outside limits under threat of violent retribution.

Big Jim Colosimo, white slaver, cabaret owner, and first of the gang chiefs of the Prohibition Era. *(Authors' Collection.)*

Johnny Torrio, Colosimo's aide, who became gangland's master organizer after Big Jim was slain in his Wabash Avenue café. *(Chicago Sun-Times Library.)*

In this first Torrio band, his protégé—variously known as Al Capone and Al Brown—was merely one such district captain, working on the West Side with such worthies as Harry "Greasy Thumb" Guzick, a white slaver, and Frankie "Millionaire Newsboy" Pope. For a while Capone and his fellow district captains did their jobs well and without rivalry. As long as William Hale "Big Bill" Thompson sat in the mayor's chair the Torrio syndicate had naught to fear from the police. In a single year the Chicago division grossed for Torrio $4,000,000 from beer peddling, $3,000,000 from gambling, $2,000,000 from prostitution, and in the suburbs the take was $4,000,000 more. Chicago had 12,000 speakeasies, beer flats, and brothels that sold illegal liquor. Police officials were paid off, and, indeed, some even helped the Torrio gang hijack trucks belonging to rivals.

But Torrio's syndicate started to disintegrate after Thompson refused to run in 1923 and a reformer named William E. Dever was elected. Under pressure, Torrio reached out for other territory and directed Al Capone to capture the western suburb of Cicero. While Torrio was on a trip to his native Italy, Capone acted; he made alliances with the local banditry, sent sluggers and killers to drive away Republicans intent on voting against his hand-picked mayoral candidate, and soon set up brothels, gambling houses, and saloons and ruled the terrorized town from armored offices in Hawthorne Inn. With Capone busy in Cicero, Torrio's subchiefs grew restlessly greedy and invaded each other's territories, hijacked trucks, slew rivals, and robbed liquor warehouses. While the horrified nation gasped, the carnage in Chicago streets continued. One of the first to go was Dion O'Banion, who dared speak ill of the six Genna brothers, rulers of a West Side kingdom of alcohol cookers; he was shot late in November 1924 by two visitors to his flower shop across from Holy Name Cathedral. In reprisal, the evil-tempered Hymie Weiss and his men surprised Torrio in front of his South Side home and shot and seriously wounded him; in the hospital a quivering Torrio told Capone, "I'm getting out, I'm going to Europe. It's all yours."

The first nickname of the man in these police identification photographs was "Snorky" and he was an errand boy and bodyguard for Torrio. He spelled his name variously: Alphonse Caponi and Al Capone, with an alias of Al Brown and another nickname of "Scarface Al." He was brought to Chicago by Torrio in 1919 and became, in time, the biggest big shot of them all. (*Authors' Collection.*)

Capone accepted the ruler's role and the warfare continued. Alliances were changed, old friends became new enemies. Three of the Gennas were slain; a young assistant state's attorney who consorted with gangsters was shot to death; Hymie Weiss himself was killed near Holy Name Cathedral less than three weeks after he had led a crazed onslaught against Capone, peppering the Hawthorne Inn with more than 1,000 bullets. Other gangsters met other kinds of death through sudden assaults on streets, in the backs of automobiles, on lonely rides. And Capone's final consolidation of his fantastic realm came on St. Valentine's Day in 1929, when his killers strode into a North Clark Street garage, lined up seven of the henchmen of Capone's last major rival, George "Bugs" Moran, and machine-gunned them to death.

Although Capone was presumably free from competition from foes, this butchery really began his downfall. He was picked up in Philadelphia

Dion O'Banion was once a singing waiter, but he was also a thief and a pickpocket and a safecracker. With the start of bootlegging, he was allied briefly with the Torrio syndicate, but broke away and became a power on the North Side, rashly carrying on warfare against the people he referred to contemptuously as "them damn Sicilians." On November 10, 1924, two men walked into O'Banion's flower shop. While one shook his hand the other shot him dead. His funeral was the gaudiest of all in gangdom's history. *(Chicago Sun-Times Library.)*

His real name was Earl Wajciechowski, but he called himself Hymie Weiss. A sullen slugger and killer, "Little Hymie" sought to avenge O'Banion's murder. He took over leadership of the O'Banion gang and sent men to kill Torrio in front of his house and Capone in Cicero. Torrio was severely wounded and fled Chicago. Unharmed, Capone assumed full chieftain's powers, met Weiss's snarling defiance by sending machine-gunners after him. Near Holy Name Cathedral one October day in 1926, Weiss stepped out of an automobile with some associates. The machine-gunners poked their weapons out of a window across the street and fired. Weiss and another man fell dead. *(Chicago Tribune Library.)*

Last of the major gang chiefs to defy Al Capone was this one-time labor racketeer and thief, George "Bugs" Moran. His band of hijackers and bootleggers was dealt a mortal blow on St. Valentine's Day in 1929. Moran himself escaped, lived on to serve prison terms for various offenses, died at sixty-five in 1957 of lung cancer in a hospital ward of the Leavenworth, Kansas, federal penitentiary. *(Chicago Sun-Times Library.)*

Symbolic pattern of Chicago in the years when gangsters ruled and slaughter on the streets was sometimes a daily occurrence. The victim with cap neatly covering his face and legs crossed is Hymie Weiss. (*Authors' Collection.*)

for carrying a gun and served ten months, emerging to find himself labeled by the federal government Public Enemy Number One. Late in the summer of 1931, after harassment by officials when he sought to live in Havana, South Dakota's Black Hills, and Los Angeles, he returned to Chicago where he was indicted for evading $215,-000 in income taxes and sentenced to serve eight years in Alcatraz Prison in San Francisco Bay. When he finally emerged, he was a victim of paresis; his mind was gone and he had spells of violence. He repaired to his $100,000 villa near Miami Beach, living out his years there lounging by his pool, fishing from a pier, and occasionally visiting with those who had become his gangland heirs in Chicago and elsewhere. When he died in 1947 the city's *Times* noted wryly that his death came a week after that of Andrew J. Volstead, father of the Prohibition Act. Noting that the effects of Caponeism in Chicago would be hard to eradicate, the editorialist aptly chided public and officialdom for their "perverse pride" in this man: "What he stood for was a 'public disgrace' because Chicago tolerated him. He became the

center of gangland pomp and power, but he was a hoodlum to whom this city paid tribute as though he were a leader by choice of the gods. . . . The city's sons who had something to offer humanity and civilization, its scientists, philosophers, writers, artists, business giants, all were second or third to the name of Capone. . . . Have we learned our lesson? There is doubt."

Curiously, in the period when Chicago was a synonym the world over for crime, corruption, and carnage, its population increased by 700,000, heading for a figure of 3,000,000 by 1930. For all his weaknesses, Big Bill Thompson was in the tradition of such boosters as Wright and Bross; where they had urged their fellow citizens to love and work for their city, Big Bill cried, "Be a Booster! Don't be a Knocker! Throw away your hammer and get a horn!" At the same time headlines told of new gang slayings, others reported new stirrings by the builders. The Chicago Plan Commission, relatively quiet during the war, became active again: "Where yesterday was the wigwam, today is the national center of population, commerce, education, music, and constructive

The St. Valentine's Day Massacre. This photograph shows six of the seven slain Moran gang members. They had been lined up by four men, two wearing police uniforms, and sprayed with machine-gun bullets. Informed of the massacre, Moran blurted, "Only Capone kills like that." (*Wide World*.)

Chief of Al Capone's machine-gun squad and the man who was believed to have led the killers on St. Valentine's Day was Vincent Gebardi, far better known as "Machine Gun" Jack McGurn. But the suave man with debonair airs furnished a strong alibi and was released by police. He continued to operate annoyingly in and around the Chicago underworld until 1936. On a February night, while quietly waiting his turn in a bowling alley on Milwaukee Avenue, he was shot in the back of the head by a man who turned and fled. (*Chicago Sun-Times Library*.)

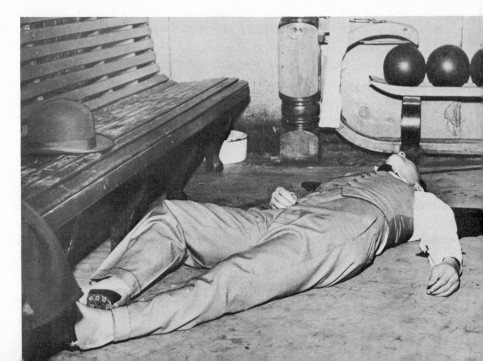

Capone's reign as premier gangster seemed assured after 1930, but actually he was started, in that year, toward his end. After serving ten months in Philadelphia, Capone came back to Chicago to ask smirkingly of Detective Chief John Stege, "You wanna see me?" Stege had no charges to place, but his men dogged Capone all over town. *(Chicago Tribune Library.)*

A decade later, after spending seven and a half years in Alcatraz for income-tax violations, Capone was still being sued in various districts—here he is leaving a Miami courtroom—for other tax delinquencies. *(Wide World.)*

Unlike those of so many of his friends and enemies, Capone's end came in bed. In his final years he suffered from the effects of paresis and had the mentality of a child. He died in his Miami Beach villa in January 1947 and was buried on a frigid and snowy day in Chicago's Mt. Olivet Cemetery. *(Mel Larson, Chicago Sun-Times.)*

art. . . . It is not too late to replace procrastination with our vigorous support of the reconstruction program. . . . Cease unnecessary bickering and get together. . . . Vim and vigor lead to victory."

Some of the builders used so much vim and vigor that the *Tribune* filed a suit against them and city officials, charging that excessive fees had been paid. Thompson made a buffoon of himself and of the city with his inane attacks on "British influences" in the city's schoolbooks and his threats to punch King George in the nose. His wildly colorful attacks on political foes brought down upon him the jeers of a nation. "Chicago is still a good deal of a Wild West town," the *St. Louis Star* was convinced, "where a soapbox showman extracting white rabbits from a gentleman's plug hat still gets a better hearing than a man in a sober suit talking business."

Yet there is rich evidence that physically the city bloomed in the agitated 1920s. Michigan Avenue, finally widened from Randolph Street to the south riverbank, with a two-deck bridge grandly stretching across the water, was now to be transformed north of the river into a modern boulevard. William Wrigley, the chewing-gum magnate, adhered closely to the Chicago Plan when he put up his two gleaming white twin skyscrapers west of the river's mouth, even to the plaza to replace a creaking and decrepit dock. The largest terra-cotta structure in the world, it

Through the wild and wicked 1920s Chicago's mayor was the boisterous and oafish William Hale "Big Bill" Thompson. He served three terms, all of them spattered with conflict and controversy. During World War I he was so pro-German before America's entry into the conflict that he was denounced as "Kaiser Bill." Corruption was rife during his postwar rule, a period also marked by his incessant clamor that his superintendent of schools was a minion of England's King George. *(Authors' Collection.)*

Crime of the Century: Nathan Leopold and Richard Loeb, in 1924, murdered a thirteen-year-old boy, were saved from hanging and sentenced to life imprisonment primarily through the forensic efforts of their lawyer, the great Clarence Darrow, seen here flanked by the two after their arraignment. Loeb was slashed to death in a Joliet penitentiary razor fight in 1936. Leopold, who established a vastly creditable record of service in prison, was paroled in February 1958, and went to Puerto Rico to work as a ten-dollar-a-month hospital attendant. *(Wide World.)*

Despite his buffooneries, Big Bill Thompson's regime witnessed the culmination of major civic improvements, some of which had been proposed in the Burnham Plan. At this dedication of the Michigan Avenue Bridge near the site of old Fort Dearborn, Thompson boosters hailed him and shrilled, "Hats off to our mayor!" *(Chicago Tribune.)*

was two years abuilding; when it was done, the city had another landmark. On the site of old Fort Dearborn up rose the London Guarantee and Accident Company Building. And across from the Wrigley Building, on the east corner of the widening Michigan Avenue north, the *Tribune* owners, after a contest in which the world's architects competed, started to erect Tribune Tower of Gothic design. Inlaid in the floor of the lobby were the words of John Ruskin: "Therefore when we build, let us think that we build forever."

One of the most complex projects in the Chicago Plan became a reality in this decade. First it was called the South Water Street Improvement, finally Wacker Drive, after the man who did so much to push it and other concepts of Dan Burnham's. As early as 1908, the Chicago Plan Commission proposed to wipe out the teeming, fantastically disorganized street where were centered the city's produce houses and replace it with a double-decked sweeping drive. Such a proposal

met with dispute, argument, and lawsuits. Ultimately, the planners won out, but not without direct legal action against those produce merchants who refused to move to a new locale. From 1924 through 1926, hundreds of workmen proceeded, building first some 600 caissons, reinforcing them with steel beams, then pouring concrete. It was a project as mighty as the raising of Lake Street in the 1850s, and equally as important to the progress of the city.

Wacker Drive finished—"They have achieved the almost impossible!" cried Mayor Dever at the dedication—it was time for new building, and more skyscrapers towered or spread themselves. Samuel Insull, the utilities magnate, built himself a 42-story Civic Opera House and near old Wolf Point, across from Wacker Drive, was erected the world's largest office building, the Merchandise Mart.

And Edgar Lee Masters, who had practiced law and written many great poems in this city,

199

Michigan Boulevard in 1924, with the Art Institute and its famous bronze lions in the foreground. In the distance are the partly finished 333 Building, covering part of the Fort Dearborn site, and the Tribune Tower, across the river. *(Kaufmann-Fabry.)*

wondered if the builders realized that their structures alone did not make a city, that "manifestly nothing can do it but the right sort of intellectual activity widely spread." This was an attitude reflected in the literary folk of the time, an anti-Philistine crowd who, like their brothers of the 1890s, deplored the spirit of materialism abroad in the town. Chicago had a Bohemia, but it was really in its final phases and the best of the writers were preparing to leave for other climes. The Renaissance that had begun in 1890 had reached its most virulent stage from 1911 to 1920 with the presence in the city of such people as Masters himself; Floyd Dell writing his novels and editing the *Friday Literary Review;* Harriet Monroe establishing her slim but influential little magazine, *Poetry;* Margaret Anderson publishing good writers and bad writers and great writers in her *Little Review,* until she fled to New York in 1917; Sherwood Anderson thriving and working and writing some of his best books; Carl Sandburg newspapering and poetizing; Harry Hansen and Keith Preston and Ben Hecht and Henry Blackman Sell and the cream of the great Henry Justin

200

Two of Chicago's most famous landmarks as they appeared when newly completed in the mid-1920s. On the left is the twin-peaked Wrigley Building, put up by the chewing-gum magnate, and on the right is Tribune Tower. *(Kaufmann-Fabry.)*

August 27, 1925, was the last day of life for this cluttered old South Water Street market. It was demolished and the produce houses shifted elsewhere to make room for the double-decked Wacker Drive. *(Chicago Tribune.)*

Work went swiftly on Wacker Drive once caissons were built. By the time this photograph was taken early in the summer of 1926, the stretch from Dearborn to Wells streets had been completed and foundations were being laid from Dearborn Street to Wabash Avenue. *(Chicago Tribune.)*

Smith's crowd at the *Daily News* jesting and debating and guffawing at Schlogl's, the literary restaurant on Wells Street. From March 1923 to June 1924 Hecht and his individualistic associate, the poet Maxwell Bodenheim, published the gaudy, ribald, and spicy journal, the *Chicago Literary Times,* but Bodenheim was already in New York, flibbertigibetting about Greenwich Village. Hecht's dedicatory editorial set the tone and indirectly revealed many creative people's attitude about the city that presumably took such childish pride in its gangsters and so little in its artists: "Chicago, the jazz baby—the reeking, cinder-ridden, joyous Baptist stronghold; Chicago,

the gum-chewing center of the world, the bleating, slat-headed rendezvous of half-witted newspapers, sociopaths, and pants makers—in the name of the Seven Holy and Imperishable Arts, Chicago salutes you! . . . The *Chicago Literary Times,* a gazette dedicated to the Sacred Ballyhoo, bumps its head thrice upon your threshold and bids you remember that Art is the watchword and Beauty the bride of the soul." Chicago did not respond, and by the middle of 1924 Hecht had gone for good to New York, where the publishers and the magazines were.

By 1926 the Chicago Renaissance, except for some valiant diehards who remained, was literally

Left. The *enfant terrible* of Chicago's literary world in the early 1920s was Ben Hecht who, with the poet Maxwell Bodenheim, published this iconoclastic and saucy newspaper. *(Authors' Collection.)*

Left. Gene Markey's caption for his caricature of Hecht: "Mr. Ben Hecht completes a series of bedtime stories for *The Youth's Companion.*" *(Gene Markey.) Right.* And Markey's caption for his deft drawing of Bodenheim: "Mr. Maxwell Bodenheim meets his favorite poet." *(Gene Markey.)*

over. Hansen left, Burton Rascoe and Sell had gone as early as 1920. Some of them continued to write or edit elsewhere, others created no longer, and for years to come one could stir lively argument about why and how the Renaissance ended, whether for economic, social, psychological, or cultural reasons. Perhaps had some of these writers remained they could have found material for vivid novels in a variety of Chicagoans who, in the last days of the 1920s and the early part of the next decade, figured in the public eye.

Such a one, for instance, was Edith Rockefeller McCormick. From her ornate mansion at 1000 Lake Shore Drive this imperious and interesting woman held the society world in a strangely fascinating spell. She had a strong will of her own, in her younger days had paid as much as $1,000,000 for a diamond dog collar and matching tiara, twice that for a pearl necklace. She invited dozens to dinner before going to the opera and timed each course with a jeweled clock so that all could leave on time. Sometimes she insisted, because she was a devout believer in reincarnation, that she was the child bride of Tutankhamen come back to life. She really was a lonely woman, for all her wealth and grandeur. She made various benefactions and hoped for public adoration. When there was no response to her gifts to the opera or to hospitals or to her plans to start a zoo on the West Side, she declared, "I want to give the public my inner motive for the founding of the Chicago Zoo Park. It is for the study of the psychology of animals. When we can make scientific deductions of the actions and reactions of animals, we will find ourselves in a position to reach the human being. We must get nearer animals to reach the human soul." Her fondest admirer, after Harold McCormick divorced her and went on to a tumultuous marriage with Ganna Walska, the opera singer, was sleepy-eyed Edwin Krenn, a young Swiss real-estate man who appeared at her door every morning with a bunch of wild flowers in his hand.

Or Samuel Insull? He rode high for decades, this British-born man of violent temper and a lover of intricate finance. Like Yerkes before him, he was deeply involved in utilities and controlled light companies, gas companies, and the streetcar lines. More than any one man, he was responsible for the abandonment of the glorious Auditorium as a center of music and opera because he had built, in an illogical place and with inferior acoustics, his own Civic Opera House at Wacker Drive and Madison Street. When the depression of 1929–30 hit the nation, Insull's various stock-holding companies tottered and collapsed. Thousands of small investors, to whom the power man had been a kind of god, lost everything. When investigations into his companies started, Insull was already in Europe; asked by Cook County's state's attorney to come back for questioning, the white-mustached old man slipped first to Florence from Paris, then to Turin, then to Athens, where he was arrested. "I have committed no crime," he told his captors. "The failure of my companies was not fraudulent. I have just been unfortunate and lost lots of money—more than $100,000,000

Samuel Insull, once virtually the most powerful man in Chicago, testifies at his trial for fraudulent use of the mails. Acquitted, he lived out the rest of his life in comparative poverty. *(Chicago Sun-Times.)*

of my own." Finally, he was driven out of Greece in 1934, captured by the Turkish government, and returned, haggard and shaky, to Chicago. He and sixteen associates went on trial for using the mails to defraud and after extended hearings he was freed. The Chicago he considered he owned paid scant heed to him now; only when he was fatally stricken with a heart attack in 1938, leaving debts of $14,000 and assets of only $1,000, did he achieve front-page treatment, and then for the last time.

Or Anton "Tony" Cermak? An immigrant boy from Bohemia, he had gone to work in the mines of southern Illinois and, coming to Chicago, had peddled kindling wood from a pushcart. A robust man with a zest for politics, he became secretary of the United Societies for Local Government, a euphemistic title for an aggregation of saloon-keepers devoted to fighting Sunday closing laws. Later, making his way up the political grades, he served as a Democratic alderman, was president of the powerful County Board, and yearned, in 1931, to be Chicago's mayor when the Century of Progress Exposition would be held in 1933. Big Bill Thompson derided him, calling him "bohunk," and urging him to go back to his pushcart. But Cermak was too strong a foe; he defeated Big Bill and pushed the man in the cowboy hat toward political oblivion. Yet Cermak's dream of being World's Fair mayor was not to be realized. After playing host to the Democratic convention in the Chicago Stadium that nominated Franklin D. Roosevelt for the presidency, Cermak, the former miner and former pushcart peddler, was invited to visit the nominee in Miami. He was with Roosevelt one warm day in 1933 when Giuseppe Zangara insanely fired shots in their direction. The bullets missed Roosevelt but struck Cermak. He lingered for a few weeks and died, and all Chicago took sorrowful pride in the words he was reported to have gasped as they carried him away, "I'm glad it was me instead of you."

In his political prime, Anton J. "Tony" Cermak, Chicago's mayor in 1932, poses with two former mayors at the Democratic national convention, Carter Harrison to his left and Edward F. Dunne. *(Chicago Sun-Times Library.)*

Equally as important to the nation—and to the world—as Lincoln's nomination for president in Chicago's Wigwam in 1860 was that of Franklin D. Roosevelt in the Chicago Stadium in 1932. Here the successful Democratic candidate receives the delegates' cheers with his wife, Eleanor, and eldest of his sons, James, on the platform with him. *(Chicago Sun-Times Library.)*

From a narrow alley at the side of the Chicago Public Library, a photographer in the early 1930s catches in his lens seventy-five years of architectural patterns, from the sunlit old-style building facing him on Randolph Street to the spire of the modern Lincoln Tower soaring upward from Wacker Drive at the rear. *(Fred J. Korth.)*

From Fair to Fair

XI

In 1933 Chicago was officially one hundred years old. And the city celebrated. On its lake shore, extending for three miles south of Soldier Field, it staged a Century of Progress Exposition, a fair whose central theme was applied science—although its most popular feature would be a blond lady who danced in the nude at the Streets of Paris—and whose exhibits and buildings comprised a display of modern, geometric design. Despite the deepening depression, the fair of 1933 made a profit, one satisfying enough to convince its promoters to hold it the following year; and after bills and expenses were paid at the end of 1934, what remained—and it was considerable— was allotted to participating cultural institutions.

In the quarter of a century since the fair—a period recorded pictorially and impressionistically in the pages that follow—Chicago underwent many surface changes but persisted in remaining a city of vivid and sharp contrasts, and its citizens continued to be among the most self-critical in the nation, yet ever ready to bark back at decriers from "the outside."

In the 1930s, after the anniversary celebrations, the city's mood remained somber. There was little building; federal works projects were more or less the prime instrument by which the city built and grew in its various aspects. There were, as in past depressions and the aftermaths, periods of bitterness and conflict, strikes, and affiliated tragedies that damaged not only the industries and workers involved but the city itself. The coming of World War II afforded the city, as had previous major wars, an opportunity to

show not only its strength but its essential frontier-town friendliness: in the war years, Chicago was the country's mightiest producer of war goods, sold more war bonds than any other city, collected more salvage materials, entertained more servicemen.

Brought to completion in the postwar years were many projects that had been planned in the 1930s, from a $40,000,000 school-building program to an expanded subway system and two huge air terminals. New forces stirred here. Industry, diversified by wartime demands, moved the city into first place in innumerable categories. At about the same time, Chicago began its development as one of the world's great medical centers, with a vast complex of hospitals and research laboratories. And it continued to maintain its premier position among all cities in steel, packing, railroads, even, despite major changes in the country's way of life, as the Number 1 city of mail-order houses and, of course, it remained the country's top convention city for organizations as diverse as the National Association of Truckers, the Ancient Exalted Order of Nobles of the Mystic Shrine and national political parties.

As ever, with the concentration on material gains came problems: racial tensions as industry lured Negro workers by the thousands from the South and insufficient housing (although agencies, both public and private, were working with zeal in the 1950s—as the population rose to nearly 6,000,000—to clear slums and improve neighborhoods) and a decrease in cultural activities (although a group of young enthusiasts organized the successful Lyric Opera) and that peculiar kind of "Chicago neurosis" which finds its leaders too often expressing enthusiasm about civic projects in their planning stages, then dawdling or delaying or quibbling.

At the same time a new breed of Booster and Boomer had arrived, as fervent about Chicago as a John Stephen Wright or a Deacon Bross of yore. They sang now of what would happen when the St. Lawrence Seaway was deepened and extended all the way to the port of Chicago by 1959, and of a new fair—the Chicago International Fair and Exposition—to be held at a refurbished Navy Pier in the summer of that year, where countries from all over the world might display their products and wares. "The fair," cried Thomas H. Coulter, head of the city's Association of Commerce and Industry, after an intercontinental whirl to 15 countries to issue invitations, "will dramatically display Chicago's new status as a city of international trade and the opportunity to become the greatest center of world trade and transportation in the western hemisphere."

Chicago's future? The future is limitless.

In 1893, the World's Columbian Exposition had its Ferris wheel. In 1933–34, Chicago's Century of Progress Exposition had its Skyride. Visitors by the many thousands lined up daily to ascend the Skyride tower—"highest man-made structure west of Manhattan"—by elevators, then be carried across the expanse of the fair in "rocket cars." Besides this popular feature, other attractions included educational and scientific and industrial exhibits and an assortment of wonders including the Midway and its many native villages, the Enchanted Island, and the Jehol Temple with goldleaf exterior costing $25,000. (*Chicago Sun-Times Library.*)

The Exposition grounds from the air. Planning for this event to mark the city's official century of life started before the depression of 1929–30. Despite the skeptics and pessimists, the fair, without governmental subsidy or civic largess, did manage to open on schedule on May 27, 1933, its light that night set off by a beam of light from the star Arcturus. The fair occupied a narrow site—on two man-made parks, Burnham and Northerly Island—along the shore of Lake Michigan stretching over 341 acres for three miles southward from Soldier Field, seen at upper left. Despite the deepening depression, the exposition made profits each year, much of it distributed to civic institutions. Its central theme was applied science. (*Kaufmann-Fabry.*)

The attraction that set visitors talking, whether they saw her or not, was the lady with the fans: Sally Rand. Born Hattie Beck twenty-eight years earlier, Sally insisted she got the idea for her sensational fan dance "from watching white herons flying in the moonlight above my grandfather's farm." In earlier years she had been an actress, art student, dancer. Shortly before the fair opened, she had the sprightly idea of appearing—and shown here—as Lady Godiva on a horse named Mike at an art students' ball. She rode down the street, but was refused permission to prance into the ball on the horse. The resultant newspaper notoriety convinced her of the publicity inherent in the stunt. When the Century of Progress Exposition opened she went to work as a fan dancer—sans any clothing—in the Streets of Paris. Such a crowd lure was Sally that 73,000 persons saw her the first month. Her salary went up from $175 to $3,000 a week, and she was off on her career as premiere danseuse of the world of fan and bubble terpsichore. Arrested many times, employed at many fairs later, she could say honestly: "I haven't been without work a day since I took off my pants." (Authors' Collection.)

209

In May 1937, at the height of the organizing drives of John L. Lewis' new labor union aggregation, then called the Congress of Industrial Organizations, some 25,000 steelworkers in the Chicago area went out on strike. One of the plants in which 1,000 nonstriking employees continued to report for duty was that of the Republic Steel Corporation in South Chicago. On that Memorial Day, several hundred strikers and sympathizers held a meeting near the plant, then began to march toward the gates to establish a picket line. As they paraded across a field, some carrying clubs and some bearing American flags, some singing and some shouting union slogans, they were met by a large force of armed policemen. A rock was thrown, cries filled the warm air. Soon there were shots and then more shots. When the uproar ceased, 10 strikers had been killed. A coroner's jury returned a verdict of justifiable homicide but a congressional investigating committee headed by Wisconsin's Senator Robert M. La Follette handed down a stern report accusing the police of starting the clash and criticizing them for using "excessive force." The event was one of the bitterest in Chicago's history between labor and capital. *(Chicago Sun-Times Library.)*

Since that tragic Memorial Day in 1937 Chicago has had other steel strikes, but it has continued to grow and develop more powerfully as the country's greatest steel producer. These twin blast furnaces at the United States Steel Corporation's South Chicago Works—one of the three major plants in the steel-producing area, along with those of the same company's at Gary and Inland Steel's at Indiana Harbor —are the world's largest; they stand 235 feet high, each with a daily capacity of 1,500 tons. Seen from a helicopter they form a backdrop for the iron-ore and limestone storage yards as well as ore-boat unloading operations. *(United States Steel Corporation.)*

In terms of dollars, Chicago's Number 1 industry is iron and steel. Combined with such subsidiary industries as machinery manufacturing and metalworking, it provides jobs for more than half a million Chicagoans. Here workmen in the casting house of an Inland Steel Company blast furnace are silhouetted against light from a flowing stream of iron as the molten metal is poured from the furnace at the left. *(Inland Steel Company.)*

Right. Consistently the world's top railroad center, Chicago's prowess in this vital field seems to be symbolized by this sleek Corn Belt Rocket of the Rock Island Lines. The twenty trunk-line railroads servicing the city operate about half of the nation's total railway mileage. As a freight hub, Chicago handles more traffic than St. Louis and New York combined. Passenger train arrivals and departures average 1,770 daily—about one every minute—and carry nearly 300,000 suburbanites and some 66,000 travelers to distant points. The city's switching area—called the Chicago Terminal District—is a network of 8,000 miles of railroad track, 208 freight terminal yards, and 225 freight houses capable of parking 207,000 railroad cars at a time. *(Kaufmann-Fabry.)*

212

Left. At Chicago's Midway Airport, the world's busiest, 14 major air lines average 900 flights a day, carry 9,000,000 passengers a year. Besides this large field some 14 miles southwest of the Loop, beyond the city's northern outskirts, there is O'Hare International Airport, whose 10-square-mile area makes it the world's largest. Besides its prominence as a rail and aviation center, Chicago has in recent years developed into the hub of the nation's trucking industry. Some 500 trucking companies provide direct and scheduled daily service to 35,000 communities in the nation. The industry, employing some 300,000 persons, provides overnight delivery service to cities inside a 400-mile radius, insures delivery to the East Coast in thirty-three hours, to the West Coast within four days. (*Metro News Photos.*)

Below. Symbol of Chicago as a wholesale distributing center is the Merchandise Mart, the world's largest commercial building. The Mart was constructed near the site of Miller's tavern (the center of the town's first business area) and was completed at a cost of $32,000,000 in 1930. Covering two city blocks, the Mart is 18 stories high, surmounted by a 25-story tower, and has a gross area of 4,023,400 square feet, almost 93 acres. Built by Marshall Field & Co., the Mart was sold in 1945 to Joseph P. Kennedy. More than 1,100 tenants line its seven and a half miles of corridors. (*William Knefel, Chicago Sun-Times.*)

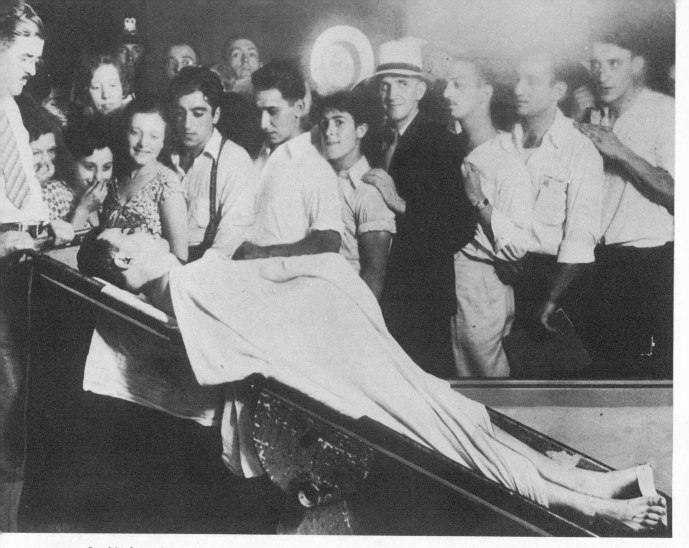

In this first of four famous Chicago photographs on these two pages, John Dillinger, the notorious swashbuckling criminal of the early 1930s, lies dead in the County Morgue, while Coroner Frank J. Walsh and a line of citizens stand gaping. After rampaging in the Middle West and other parts of the country, Dillinger was slain by Federal agents and local police as he strolled out of a Chicago movie theater on the warm night of July 22, 1934. *(Swain Scalf and William Loewe, Chicago Tribune.)*

Wendell Willkie blazes with irate indignation after he is spattered with eggs by an uninhibited Chicagoan. The incident occurred on October 23, 1940, during Willkie's election campaign against President Roosevelt when the Republican candidate arrived at the La Salle Street Station. The *Chicago Times* published the remarkable photograph on page one, along with this statement by its editor, Richard J. Finnegan: "Deepest apologies to you, Mr. Willkie. The whole town is genuinely sorry and ashamed for the action of this single ONE of its three-and-a-half million citizens." *(Borrie Kanter, Chicago Sun-Times.)*

In April 1944, the huge mail-order firm of Montgomery Ward and Company was involved in rancorous controversy with the United States Government. When its board chairman, Sewell Avery, refused to obey commands of the War Labor Board because he contended his company was not involved in war work, the plant was ordered seized. On the morning of April 27, Avery came to his office as usual, declined to leave. So the officer in charge of the soldiers stationed at the mail-order house sent two of his men to lift the firm-minded Avery out of his chair and carry him outside, a remarkable event recorded here. *(William Pauer, Chicago Sun-Times.)*

After years of having its own opera companies, Chicago experienced a period when its opera was furnished by visiting troupes. Then in 1954 the Lyric Opera Company was organized, with its star, the lustrous Maria Meneghini Callas, making her American debut. She loved Chicago and Chicago loved her, but on the night of November 17, 1955, as she finished a performance of *Madame Butterfly,* she was greeted in the wings of the Opera House by seven deputy United States marshals, one of whom, Ralph Pringle, sought to serve her with a summons for a hearing in a contract dispute. Madame Callas' reaction—and Pringle's—was vividly captured by a newsman's camera. Calling Chicagoans "Zulus," the diva fled, but returned in subsequent opera and concert seasons to regain public adulation. *(Bud Daley, Chicago Daily News.)*

Artist Gary Sheahan's conception of a momentous day in the history of Chicago—and of the universe. On December 2, 1942, Nobel Prize-winning physicist Enrico Fermi and a group of his associates and coworkers gathered on a balcony close to a uranium pile imbedded in a matrix of graphite on a squash court under the west stands of the University of Chicago's Stagg Field. That afternoon they knew their efforts had been successful: The first self-sustaining chain reaction had been achieved and the controlled release of nuclear energy had been initiated, ushering in the Atomic Age. *(Chicago Tribune.)*

The nation's senior atomic-energy research and development installation is Argonne National Laboratory, twenty-five miles from the heart of the city. Most of the work done here deals with peace-time applications of atomic energy. Some 1,700 scientists, engineers, and technicians carry on their duties in 97 buildings spread over a 3,700-acre tract of land. Argonne's facilities are valued at more than $85,500,000. This is a view of a pool looking down, showing an irradiation rack with fuel elements in place and a fuel element carrier with lid removed. *(Argonne National Laboratory.)*

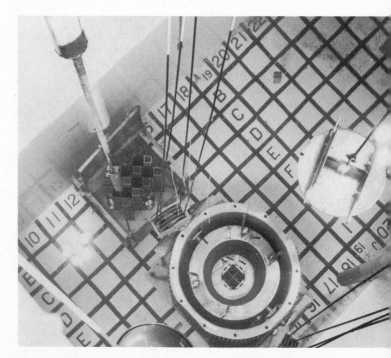

216

The trek to the suburbs in recent years has been steady and vigorous, in some cases resulting in population increases in outlying districts of more than 150 per cent. To get there, motorists use Chicago's express drives, inevitably winding up—when, as shown here, the famous and changeable Chicago weather shifts suddenly—in traffic jams and creep-by-creep travel homeward. *(Louis Giampa, Chicago Sun-Times.)*

For generations Chicagoans talked and dreamed about a speedy thoroughfare from the city toward the West. Daniel Burnham, in his Chicago Plan of 1908, called Congress Street the "Axis of Chicago" and proposed transforming it into an expressway. Not until 1944, after years of wrangling over appropriations and myriad details, did work on this project actually start; it was first opened to traffic in 1956, handling within a year as many as 50,000 cars a day heading to western suburbs. Its cost: $150,000,000. *(Arthur Shay.)*

Above. As in most big American cities, there is a Skid Row in Chicago, centering on West Madison Street, just off the Loop, and stretching into surrounding avenues, where derelicts loaf, lounge, and sleep off drinking bouts. *(Arthur Shay.)* And by vivid contrast Chicago has its famous Glass Houses *(below left)* on Lake Shore Drive and the stainless-steel Inland Steel Company Building *(below right). (Hedrich-Blessing.)*

219

Above. Chicago, about 2058. In a contest sponsored by Carson, Pirie, Scott and Company, four fledgling architects in their twenties and their thirty-five-year-old instructor won $20,000 for their imaginative plan for Chicago one hundred years hence. Main feature of their layouts, one of which, looking toward the lake from the southwest, is shown above, is the concept of maintaining the Loop's concentration of economic, social, and civic life with fewer large buildings and larger areas for parks and malls. *(Carson, Pirie, Scott and Company.)*

Left. The river that flows backward. A striking scene, looking westward at dusk, of the Chicago River and its bridges. *(Fred J. Korth.)*

Above. Another view of the Chicago River, as a boat might see the city approaching it from Lake Michigan. On the left is a sector of the Outer Drive, with the city's tallest building, the Prudential, at extreme left, and directly ahead are such other landmarks as Tribune Tower, the Wrigley Building, the 333 Building, and the new Chicago Sun-Times Building. *(William Winek, Chicago Sun-Times.) Right.* Symbol of the Future. A Norwegian freighter docks in the Chicago River, with the giant Prudential Building in the background. In years to come, with the completion of the St. Lawrence Seaway and new Chicago docks, harbors and port facilities, the numbers of such ships and others from foreign lands are expected to multiply many times over, fulfilling the generations-old predictions that Chicago will one day be a gigantic center of world trade. *(Robert MacKay.)*

Below. In 1957 two men who had contributed much to Chicago were brought back for symposia and discussions in connection with a "Chicago Dynamic" Program. Frank Lloyd Wright (left), the genius of architecture, proposed a skyscraper a mile high, decentralization of the city, and a wholesale movement of citizens to the city's green outskirts. Carl Sandburg, the city's unofficial poet laureate, admitted he was as excited about Chicago as he had been as a youth: "I will never tire of the lake. I will never tire of Michigan Avenue and the Outer Drive . . ." *(Archie Lieberman.)*

Index

Addams, Jane, 154, 156, 167, 190
Ade, George, 161
Adler, Dankmar, 151-52, 154
Albany Journal, 81
Allouez, Father Claude, 38-39, 46
Altgeld, John Peter, 149-50, 168
American Railway Union, 167, 171
Ames, Mrs. Fred, 180
Anarchy and Anarchists, 139, 147-49
Anderson, Margaret, 200
Anderson, Sherwood, 200
Andreas, A. T., 127, 132
Anshuts, Carl, 23
Appleton's Journal, 105
Arbeiter Zeitung, 146
Argonne National Laboratory, 216
Armour, Philip Danforth, 136, 178
Armstrong, Maitland, 164
Arnold, C. D., 165
Arnold, Isaac Newton, 122-23
Art Institute of Chicago, 7, 139, 151, 157, 159, 161, 200
Astor, John Jacob, 63, 153
Authors' Collection, 73, 104, 168, 174-75, 179, 192-93, 195, 198, 202, 209
Avery, Sewell, 215

Baird, W. B., 92
Ballou, Miss Addie, 102
Ballou's Pictorial Drawing Room Companion, 10, 35
Barker, Charles, 28
Baughman, Miss Elizabeth, 7
Bayne, Beverly, 183
Beaubien, Jean B., 63, 66-67, 79
Beaubien, Mark, 65-67, 69, 75, 89
Beery, Wallace, 183
Bellin, N., 42
Bennett, Edward H., 187
Bennett, Frank I., 187
Benson, Joseph, 7
Bentley, Cyrus, 22
Bernhardt, Sarah, 137, 142
Besant, Sir Walter, 160
Bodenheim, Maxwell, 202
Bradley, Hezekiah, 63
Breese, Sidney A., 82
Bremer, Fredrika, 19
Bronco Billy, 183
Bross, William, 16, 81-82, 85, 89, 118, 130-31, 195, 207
Brown, John, 30

Brown, William H., 114
Buchanan, James, 20, 92
Buffalo Bill, 167
Burnham, Daniel C., 152, 162-63, 167, 187, 189-90, 199, 217
Burns, Miss Marjorie, 180
Burroughs, Rev. J. C., 160
Bushman, Francis X., 183

Calhoun, John, 72, 78
Callas, Maria Meneghini, 215
Capone, Al, 192-97
Carbutt, J., 122, 132
Carleton, Will, 102
Carnegie, Andrew, 108
Carson Pirie Scott & Co., 107, 220
Cass, Lewis, 63, 65-66
Catlin, Miss Irene, 180
Caton, Mrs. Della, 180
Caton, John D., 73-74
Century Magazine, 146, 164, 166
Cermak, Anton J., 204
Chandonmai, 60
Chapin, John B., 117
Chappel, Elizabeth, 68, 70, 72
Charlevoix, Father, 42
Chicago American, 73, 75, 78
Chicago and Alton Railroad, 138
Chicago and Its Makers, 201
Chicago & North Western, 37, 86-87
Chicago Antiquities, 11, 41-42
Chicago Daily News, 160, 202, 215
Chicago Democrat, 72-74, 78-79
Chicago Evening Journal, 101
Chicago Evening Post, 120
Chicago's Great Century, 117
Chicago Herald, 30, 190
Chicago Historical Society, 7, 11, 15, 17-20, 22-27, 33, 39, 41, 43-44, 48, 51, 54, 56-57, 59-60, 64, 67-69, 71-74, 76-77, 79, 81-82, 84-85, 90-91, 95-98, 101, 104-5, 109-11, 113-14, 116, 123, 129, 132, 142, 144, 180, 182
Chicago Literary Times, 202
Chicago Magazine, 33, 64
Chicago Municipal Reference Library, 7, 125
Chicago Plan Commission, 189, 195, 199
Chicago Public Library, 7, 27, 58-60, 65, 70, 78, 94, 102, 111, 121, 136-38, 205

Chicago Sun-Times, 7, 80, 121, 124, 135-36, 140, 143, 146-47, 150, 154-56, 158, 161, 168-69, 173, 191-92, 194, 196-97, 203-5, 207, 210, 213-15, 217, 219, 221
Chicago Then and Now, 164
Chicago Times, 99, 104, 195, 214
Chicago Times-Herald, 160
Chicago Tribune, 4, 7, 13, 73, 83, 89, 99, 101, 103, 120, 126, 133, 135-36, 140, 143, 156, 159-61, 172-74, 176, 179-80, 188-89, 194, 197, 199-201, 214, 216, 221
Cincinnati Inquirer, 11
Claflin, Tennessee, 105
Clark, George Rogers, 46-47
Cleveland, Grover, 167
Cleveland Plain Dealer, 11
Codman, Henry, 164
Cole, George E., 179
Collier's, 175
Colosimo, "Big" Jim, 192
Comiskey, Charles, 185
Cook, Daniel P., 65-66, 71
Copelin and White, 128
Corning, Erastus, 80
Corwin, Tom, 80
Couch, Ira, 24, 31, 80
Couch, James, 80
Coughlin, John, 168-69, 174-76
Coulter, Thomas C., 207
Coxey, "General" Jacob, 167
Cregier, E. B., 186
Crosby, Uranus B., 103
Curie, William H., 24

Daily Democrat, 11, 19
Daley, Bud, 215
Daley, Richard J., 219
Dana, Charles A., 162
Darrow, Clarence, 198
Davis, George, 64
Davis, Jefferson, 70
Davis, Theodore R., 128
Davis, Thomas V., 75, 78
Dean, Grant, 7
Dearborn, General Henry, 50
Debs, Eugene Victor, 167-68, 171
De Castelnau, Francis, 64
Delane, John, 10
De L'Isle, William, 42
Dell, Floyd, 200
Dever, William E., 193, 199

Dial, 162
Dillinger, John, 214
Dole, George W., 74, 76, 78, 111
Douglas, Stephen A., 19-21, 23, 28-29, 75, 81-82, 89, 92, 95, 104, 160
Dreiser, Theodore, 160, 174
Drew, Lillian, 183
Dunne, Edward F., 204
Dunne, Finley Peter, 160-61
Du Sable, Jean Baptiste, 50, 59

Earle, Lawrence C., 43, 51, 74
Edison, Thomas, 164
Ellsworth, Colonel Elmer E., 94
Engel, George, 148
Everleigh sisters, 174, 176-79

Fairbank, N. Kellogg, 176
Farnum, Henry, 114
Fawkes, Joseph W., 30
Fergus, George H., 54
Fermi, Enrico, 216
Field, Eugene, 160-61
Field, Marshall, 106, 118, 127, 131, 139, 153, 155, 159, 180, 188, 213
Fielden, Samuel, 146-47, 149, 150
Finnegan, Richard J., 214
Fischer, Adolph, 148
Fletcher, Ralph Seymour, 62
Foot, Starr, 80
Formes, Karl, 23
Foy, Eddie, 182-83
Franquelin, Jean P. Louis, 41
Freelove, Julia, 22
Friday Literary Review, 200
Frink, John, 79
Frontenac, Count, 40, 42
Fuller, Henry Blake, 160

Gage, Lyman J., 136, 171
Garland, Hamlin, 160
Gary, Judge Joseph, 150
Gates, Frederick T., 159
Genna brothers, 193
Geraldine, Dion, 164
Giampa, Louis, 217
Gillette, William, 183
Glass, F. R., 59
Gleason, Frederick Grant, 159
Goldman, Emma, 150
Goodspeed, Thomas W., 159
Graham, Ernest, 164
Grant, Ulysses S., 104
Gravier, Father Jacques, 46
Greeley, Horace, 80
Gross Cyclorama, 118, 123
Guerin, Jules, 187
Gunther, Charles F., 144
Guzick, Harry, 193

Haines, John C., 14, 31
Half Century's Progress of the City of Chicago, 152
Hamilton, General Henry, 46-47
Hansen, Harry, 200, 203
Harper, William Rainey, 159-60
Harper's New Monthly Magazine, 141

Harper's Weekly, 10, 24, 26, 92-93, 119-20, 127-28, 151, 165, 170-71
Harrison, Carter Henry (the younger, and older), 137, 140, 142, 147, 154, 165, 169, 174, 176, 179, 192, 204
Harrison, William Henry, 48
Heald, Nathan, 56, 58, 59, 61
Heald, Mrs. Nathan, 60, 62
Healy, George P. A., 23, 30
Hecht, Ben, 200, 202
Hedrich-Blessing, 218
Helm, Linai T., 56, 58-59, 61
Helm, Mrs. Margaret, 60-62
Hennepin, Father Louis, 44
Herrick, Robert, 160
Hesler, A., 11, 13, 15, 17-20, 23, 28, 91
Hewitt, Herbert, 7
Hoffman Collection, 185
Holabird, John, 152
Horton, D. H., 126
Hubbard, G. S., 63, 67, 69, 74-75, 77-78
Hunt, Richard, 153, 166
Hunt's Merchants' Magazine, 10
Hutchinson, Charles L., 161

Illinois Bell Telephone, 141, 181
Illinois Central, 35-36, 68, 82, 90, 100-1, 113, 120
Illinois State Historical Society, 7, 41, 45, 97
Inland Steel Co., 211, 218
Insull, Samuel, 199, 203-4
International Publishing Co., 152

Jay, John, 50
Jenney, Wm. Le Baron, 150, 152, 154
Jevne and Almini Prints, 90, 107, 112
Johnson, Lathrop, 79
Johnson, William, 53
Jolliet, Louis, 33, 38-41
Joutel, Henri, 44
Judd, Norman, 91

Kanter, Borrie, 214
Kaufmann-Fabry, 7, 55, 111, 139, 160, 184, 188, 200, 208, 212
Keating, William H., 63, 65
Kelly, Ed, 219
Kenna, Michael, 168-70, 174-76
Kennedy, Joseph P., 213
Kennelly, Martin J., 219
Kerfoot, William D., 127, 131
Kinzie, John, 39, 52-53, 56-59, 61-63
Kipling, Rudyard, 157
Kirkland, Caroline, 16, 21
Kirkland, Joseph, 126
Knefel, William, 213
Korth, Fred J., 205, 220
Krausz, Sigmund, 163
Krenn, Edwin, 203

Ladies' Journal, 25
Laflin, Matthew, 19
LaFollette, Robert M., 210
Lakeside Monthly, 134
Land Owner Magazine, 130

Langtry, Lily, 143
Lardner, Ring, 183
Larson, Mel, 197
La Salle, 40, 42, 44-45
Lawrence, George R., 172
Lawrence, James, 20-21
Leiter, Levi Z., 106, 118, 122, 127, 131, 139
Leopold, Nathan, 198
Leslie, Alexander, 19, 23
Leslie's Weekly, 19, 22, 32
Lewis, John L., 210
Lieberman, Archie, 220
Lincoln, Abraham, 20, 23, 28, 89, 91-94, 96, 98-101, 114, 205
Lingg, Louis, 149
"Little Egypt," 165, 167-68
Little Review, 200
Loeb, Richard, 198
Loewe, William, 214
London Times, 10
Louis XIV, 38, 44

McClernand, General John A., 98
McCormick, C. H., 10, 34, 81, 93, 101, 146
McCormick, Edith Rockefeller, 203
McCormick, Harold, 203
McCormick, Leander, 110
McCormick, Medill, 180
McCormick, R. H., 110-11, 122
McCormick, Robert R., 180
McCutcheon, John T., 161, 175
McDonald, Mike, 140
McGurn, Jack, 196
McKim, Charles, 164
McNally, Thomas, 175
MacKay, Robert, 221
MacVeagh, Franklin, 180
Madsen, Al, 4
Maes, Nicolas, 45
Markey, Gene, 202
Marquette, Father Jacques, 39-41, 43
Masters, Edgar Lee, 199-200
Martineau, Harriet, 77
Mason, Roswell B., 101, 118, 125-26
Maynard, George, 164
Medill, Joseph, 83, 126, 131, 133, 180
Membre, Father Zenobus, 42
Mencken, H. L., 160
Meserve Collection, 28
Metro News Photos, 213
Miller, Samuel, 64
Millett, Frank D., 164
Monroe, Harriet, 200
Montgomery Ward and Co., 181, 215
Moody, Dwight L., 22, 162
Moody, Walter D., 187
Moran, George, 193-94, 196
Morris, Nelson, 136
Mover, Albert, 98
Mulligan, Colonel James A., 95
Mumford, Lewis, 190

Neebe, Oscar W., 149
Newberry Library, 7, 32, 64, 103, 128
Newberry, Oliver, 74, 76, 78
Newberry, Walter L., 111

New York Central Railroad, 80
New York Daily News, 180
New York Illustrated News, 90
New York Public Library, 7, 40, 83
New York Sun, 162
New York Times, 7
New York Tribune, 80
Nickerson, Samuel J., 155
Nicolet, Jean, 38
Nocerino, Larry, 219
Norris, Frank, 158, 160
Norris' Directory, 76

O'Banion, Dion, 193-94
Ogden, Mahlon D., 123, 128
Ogden, William B., 16, 31, 75, 77-82, 85, 87, 99, 111
O'Leary, Mr. & Mrs. P., 115-16, 124
Ouilmette, Antoine, 50, 59, 74
Ourand, Charles H., 56
Owsley, Harry Bryan, 179

Palmatary, I. T., 4
Palmer, John, 126
Palmer, Potter, 22, 25, 29, 88, 100, 106, 114, 150, 154-5
Parkman, Francis, 41
Parsons, Albert R., 146, 148, 150
Partridge, Black, 58-60
Patterson, J. Medill & Eleanor, 180
Patti, Adelina, 154
Pauer, William, 215
Paulist Fathers, 21, 70
Peck, F. W., 31, 72, 78, 154
Pickett, Montgomery B., 164
Pierce, Dr. Bessie Louise, 7
Pinet, Father Pierre, 44
Pinkerton, Allan, 98, 146
Plumbe, Jr., John, 72
Poetry, 200
Polk, James Knox, 80
Pope, Frankie, 193
Pope, Nathaniel, 66, 89
Popple, Henry, 42
Post, George B., 164
Prairie Farmer, 73, 78
Press and Tribune, 25, 30
Preston, Keith, 200
Pringle, Ralph, 215
Pullman, George M., 14, 24, 108, 167

Quaife, Milo, 7

Rand, Sally, 209
Rascoe, Burton, 203
Ray, Charles, 83
Reinhart, C. S., 119
Remington, Frederick, 171
Republic Steel Corp., 210
Rhymer, Mrs. Mary Frances, 7
Rice, Colonel Edward, 164
Rice, John Blake, 29, 84
Rice, Wallace, 161
Richard, Richard, 4, 112
Ridpath, John Clark, 157, 160
Riis, Jacob, 187
Robinson, A., 57, 60, 62, 64, 74, 113
Rockefeller, John D., 159-60
Roebuck, Alva W., 181

Rogers, W. A., 171
Rohl-Smith, Carl, 60
Ronan, Ensign George, 60-61
Roos, R., 41
Roosevelt, Eleanor, 205
Roosevelt, Franklin D., 204-5, 214
Roosevelt, James, 205
Root, George F., 126
Root, John Wellborn, 152, 161
Rosenwald, Julius, 181
Rosenwald Museum, 165
Rovington, W. W., 28
Rumsey, A. G., 70
Ruskin, John, 199
Russell, J. B. F., 77, 81

St. Cyr, Father John M. I., 21, 70, 72
St. Gaudens, Augustus, 164
St. Louis Post, 11
St. Louis Star, 197
Sachs, Morris B., 219
Sandburg, Carl, 200, 220
Sankey, Ira D., 162
Sawyer, Miss Elaine, 7
Scalf, Swain, 214
Scammon, J. Young, 31
Schaack, Michael, 147, 150
Schnaubelt, Rudolph, 149
Scholl, Walter, 7, 176-78
Schoolcraft, Henry R., 39, 63
Schwab, Michael, 149
Scribner's Monthly, 145
Sears, Roebuck and Co., 181
Sell, Henry Blackman, 200, 203
Seward, William H., 89, 91
Shaw, George Bernard, 150
Shaw, Vic, 178
Shay, Arthur, 217-18
Sheahan, Gary, 47, 216
Shock, Bigford and Co., 126
Sinclair, Patrick, 50
Sinclair, Upton, 137
Sloan's Weekly, 24
Smith, Gipsy, 178
Smith, Henry Justin, 200-2
Spies, August R., 146-48, 150
Spoor, George K., 183, 186
Starr, Allen Gates, 154
Stead, William T., 170-71
Stege, John, 197
Stein, Jr., Eugene I., 7
Steiner, Arnold, 30
Storey, Wilbur Fisk, 99, 104
Stowe, Mrs. Harriet Beecher, 22
Stratton Collection, 183
Strayer, Paul, 45, 52, 57
Streeter, George W., 176, 182
Street Types of Chicago, 163
Stuart, William, 78
Sturgis & Buckingham, 113
Sullivan, L. H., 151-52, 154, 157, 165-67
Swanson, Gloria, 183
Swearingen, James S., 51-52
Sweeney, Thomas S., 120
Swift, Gustavus F., 136
Szarkowski, John, 152

Taylor, J. W., 158

Thomas, T., 122, 139, 157, 161
Thompson, James, 68
Thompson, Lydia, 104
Thompson, William Hale, 189, 193, 195, 197-99, 204
Todd, John, 46
Tonti, Henri, 42, 44-45
Toothe, William, 23-24
Torrio, Johnny, 192-94
Townsend, Fred C., 135
Train, George Francis, 110
Tree, Lambert, 122
Trowbridge, W. E. S., 67, 81
Tuckerman, Fred, 185
Turpin, Ben, 183
Tuttle, Nelson and Henry, 114

United States Steel Corp., 211
University of Chicago, 7, 159-60, 162, 165, 216
University of Minnesota Press, 152

Van Brunt, Henry, 164
Vanderbilt, William H., 153
Van Osdel, John, 29, 122, 133
Van Voorhis, Dr. Isaac, 56, 61
Varnum, Jacob, 63
Volk, Leonard W., 23, 29
Volstead, Andrew J., 195
Von Schneidnau, F., 82

Wacker, Charles H., 187, 199
Walker, Martin O., 79
Walsh, Frank J., 214
Walska, Ganna, 203
Ward, A. Montgomery, 157, 181
Ward, William, 146-47
Watson, Carrie, 171
Water, James, 30
Wayne, General Anthony, 48-49, 52
Weed, Thurlow, 80-81, 89, 91
Wells, William, 48, 59, 61
Weiss, Hymie, 193-95
Wentworth, John, 11, 14-16, 22, 78-80, 85, 88, 95
Whistler, John, 51-54, 56
Whitehead, Henry, 72
Whitlock, Brand, 161
Wide World, 167, 196-98
Wilde, Oscar, 142
Willard, Miss Francis L., 70
Willing, Henry J., 155
Willkie, Wendell, 214
Winek, William, 221
Wood, Colonel Joseph H., 112
Woodhull, Victoria, 105
Wright, Frank Lloyd, 220
Wright, J. S., 16, 34, 68-70, 72-73, 75, 78, 89, 99, 126, 131, 195, 207
Wrigley, William, 197, 200, 221

Yale, 159
Yerkes, Charles Tyson, 164, 169-70, 174, 176, 179, 203
Y.M.C.A., 22, 162
Youth's Companion, 202

Zangara, Giuseppe, 204